Iona Abbey Cookbook

L to R: Anja Jardine, Annie Sharples, Cameron Newell, Janina Bößert, Willemien Wierenga-Bremmer

Iona Abbey Cookbook

Anja Jardine

wild goose
publications

www.ionabooks.com

First published 2023 by
Wild Goose Publications
Suite 9, Fairfield, 1048 Govan Road, Glasgow G51 4XS, Scotland
A division of Iona Community Trading CIC
Limited Company Reg. No. SC156678
www.ionabooks.com

ISBN 978-1-80432-250-5
Cover and internal photos © Anja Jardine

Overseas distribution
Australia: Willow Connection Pty Ltd, 1/13 Kell Mather Drive,
Lennox Head, NSW 2478
New Zealand: Pleroma, Higginson Street, Otane 4170, Central Hawkes Bay

Printed by Bell & Bain, Thornliebank, Glasgow

MIX
Paper from
responsible sources
FSC
www.fsc.org   FSC® C007785

The Abbey Kitchen

This book has its roots in the high-ceilinged, bright and well-equipped kitchen of Iona Abbey – a place steeped in history and stories. Run by the Iona Community (see next chapter), this kitchen has been home to many cooks since the Abbey's restoration which started with Rev George MacLeod in 1938.

Most of us chefs, past and present, have had no formal training but have brought enthusiasm and drive to learn on the job. Kitchen environments are busy, often stressful, and the work is both challenging and rewarding.

Working tirelessly with us over the decades have been countless volunteers. People of all ages, from different backgrounds and religions, from all over the world, have joined us, bringing expertise, spirit and energy. Without their hard work, running this place would not have been possible.

It is the encouragement of many of the staff I have worked with, and lots of guests who have enjoyed our food, that has made me write this book.

The following recipes are a collection for all-week cooking – nothing particularly fancy, but good, honest, healthy food, with some sugary treats. Most of them are Abbey favourites which you would find being served from large dishes to groups of people sharing food and community around the big oak refectory tables here.

Welcome to Iona Abbey Kitchen.

Contents

The Iona Community   8
A little bit about the Cook   10
Food in a changing world   11
About the recipes   14
On equipment   16
On suppliers of ingredients   17

Breakfast!   18

Bread   20

Sandwich spreads   28

Soups   31

Salads   51

Vegetarian main courses   72

Fish and seafood   108

Meat   118

Vegetable side dishes   127

Sweet treats   132

Drinks   162

Thank you!   166
Books mentioned in the recipes   167

The Iona Community

Bread and justice

O God,
to those who are hungry, give bread
and – to those who have bread –
give a hunger for justice.

(A grace often used in the Abbey)

The Iona Community came into being through the rebuilding of an ancient Abbey, the work of a mixture of people concerned about poverty, injustice and the breakdown of community in the places where they lived, and in the wider world.

That's still the focus of this radical Christian movement. We are sustained by faith, commitment and by companionship – which literally means sharing meals. At the Abbey and MacLeod Centre on Iona, the Camas Centre on Mull, and wherever we meet in the Community's Family Groups (cell groups), food keeps us going – and is definitely something to be enjoyed! Gathered round the Refectory tables in the Abbey, folk – volunteers, staff and the guests who come each week – look forward to good, simple food, in meals that build community.

At this point I want to name my favourite soups, with wholesome ingredients and surprising spices, or linger over a description of the fragrance and taste of freshly-baked bread. However, I know that Anja's recipes that follow will do that for you – stimulate your imagination and your taste-buds – with practical advice to take into your own kitchen.

What I can do here is draw attention to the way she writes about food, with a mixture of enjoyment and ethical discernment. She draws on her own childhood on the other side of the Iron Curtain, to remind us that food should never be taken for granted. In Britain now, an increasing number of people are living in poverty – with poor housing, low income, unaffordable fuel bills and more and more families going hungry. The cheapest food on offer in the supermarkets is often the least nutritious. But who can blame those who buy it? So, living with austerity that's the result of government policies, one reaction is rage at unfairness – but another (which you will find here) is a celebration of simple nutritious food which is affordable.

Anja's budgeting and buying for the Abbey kitchen includes choosing local ingredients wherever possible, not only to reduce food-miles but because fresh food tastes better and local producers are supported. Fair Trade is taken seriously too, organic farming, animal welfare and a variety of plant-based recipes. Being true to our Community aim of living simply and well on this Earth means that these are realistic, not elitist, choices. Sometimes the costs will still be very challenging for a Community cook on a shoestring. This keeps us in touch with the reality of many of our fellow citizens.

So Anja and her volunteers in the Abbey kitchen, making the most of the best natural ingredients they can source, and wasting nothing, rise to that challenge and produce – meal after meal – food to enjoy. Try it!

Jan Sutch Pickard

A little bit about the Cook

I love food. I love feeding people. I love eating.

The whole process of planning a meal, making it, alone or with other people, and sharing it with family and friends makes me happy.

I grew up in Eastern Germany, in a small Saxon village near Leipzig. In my family, food was about nourishment after a long day at work, or about celebrating festivals or anniversaries. Meals were around the big table. I fondly remember all the big family celebrations with tables laden with cakes or cold meats, cheeses and salads, people of all ages chatting away loudly.

While most of our food wasn't fancy, it was home-made, healthy and plentiful. We had a big vegetable garden, and once a year we slaughtered a pig (yes, I did help with the proceedings) which provided us with plenty of meat in the shape of sausages, puddings, frozen cuts, preserved pâtés in jars. The wee village shop offered the rest we needed.

After the fall of the wall, I was lucky enough to spend a week on Iona, staying at the Iona Community's MacLeod Centre. It might just have been the impressionable age of 17 or the realisation that I had found a place that was more than just a holiday destination – whatever – I knew I wanted to come back.

I did, for shorter stays as a backpacker, camping at the North End (eating – and loving! – processed cheese slices on soft white bread, being on a restricted student budget), and then in 1999 as a volunteer for the Iona Community. I spent most of that season working in the then still-existing coffee house and in both of the Abbey and MacLeod Centre kitchens, realising that I very much enjoyed cooking as a job – more than that, really loved it and wanted to do more of it. Having just spent the previous five years doing a business studies degree at university back in Germany (not too enthusiastically) I had known for some time that I wouldn't find pleasure working in an office.

I became the Abbey Cook in February 2000 and have been a chef ever since, learning on the job at the Abbey, in the Argyll Hotel and at the St Columba Hotel.

Back at the Abbey since 2008 I still think there is no better occupation for me out there.

Anja Jardine, Abbey Cook, Spring 2023

Food in a changing world

People have been cooking food ever since the domestication of fire over 300,000 years ago. Cooking aided digestion, increased our calorie intake, made food safer and opened up new food sources. Some scientists believe that it was the ability to roast or boil hard-to-digest foods like wheat, rice, potatoes and meat, today's staples, and the connected increase of calorie intake, that enabled our brains to grow bigger and set us on the way to become the powerful and intelligent species we are today.

While eating is necessary for survival, food is much more than just a source of fuel for our bodies. In most cultures, for many people, food has been and still is the basis of family and communal life, of hospitality. Eating connects and comforts people; it is a big part of celebrations and traditions; it gives our days routine, a pattern; it creates jobs and places of welcome. The right food can heal, physically and mentally, and open us up to new experiences.

Both cooking and eating are sensual experiences of seeing, smelling, hearing and touching. We find pleasure in the crunch of biting into a juicy apple, the smell of onions frying, the colours of fruit and vegetables on a market stall, the feel of warm custard on our tongue.

Beautiful images – but does everybody really feel like this? Does everybody have the luxury of experiencing food as a pleasure? Is eating making us healthy and happy? Are we spending time on careful shopping for ingredients and the cooking of healthy and satisfying food?

Here in Britain, and in other countries all over the world, we are challenged with the deep divide between rich and poor, the weak and the powerful. This is a gap which seems to be ever growing, whether we are talking about parents who, faced with frequent cuts to the welfare system, skip meals to enable their children to eat, or small farmers or grocery shops struggling to survive in the face of big global companies which control whole markets.

In 2019, according to a report of the Food and Agriculture Organisation of the United Nations, 690 million people, 8.9% of the world population, were undernourished. Food insecurity, caused by conflict and natural disasters, has been on the rise in the past years and the outlook, if we continue with our slow and often inefficient reactions to climate change, is bleak.

The food industry itself, especially industrialised animal farming, is a big culprit in global warming, responsible for 30% of greenhouse gas emissions and 70% of freshwater use. Deforestation and other land conversion for food production is the main cause of biodiversity loss.

At the same time as people go hungry, we are also seeing an acute increase in obesity in all cultures and layers of society. It would be far too simplistic to blame a high food intake and lack of physical activity for this epidemic – scientists now know that while genes, environment and eating behaviour play a role, it is our gut microbes, and how we treat and feed them, that have the most influence on our weight and wellbeing. (See some very interesting reading in Tim Spector's *The Diet Myth*.)

Another challenge we are faced with is the decline of home cooking and the resulting loss of cooking traditions and skills being passed down from generation to generation. This trend has long been encouraged by the processed food industry, who in their advertising make cooking seem a slog, an old-fashioned thing: 'If you are modern, buy our food, don't waste your time in the kitchen!' These companies have a vested interest in destroying the home food culture. They want people to buy their often cheaper than home-cooked produce, which because of its high salt, sugar and fat content is addictive and very unhealthy.

We also live in a society where paid employment is valued more than the traditional role of the home-maker, where people work and commute for long hours. While costs of ingredients have decreased, cooking shows achieve high viewing figures and our shelves are full of the latest cookbooks, cooking itself has for many become a mere weekend hobby.

There is a temptation to be critical of people who repeatedly feed themselves and their families ready-made, often highly processed, food. However we all know the pressures and restraints people face when juggling commuting, full time jobs and family life.

While nobody will be able to address the above challenges and make changes overnight, we all can do our little bit to combat food injustice, climate change, eating-related health issues and the loss of cooking skills and traditions.

According to a report by the EAT Lancet Commission, 'food is the single strongest lever to optimise human health and environmental sustainability on Earth'. For Western countries it suggests a sustainable diet that is mainly plant-based, supplemented with some meat, dairy and fish from responsibly reared or sourced animals.

As individuals we can't solve all these problems. But as consumers, in practice, this could mean:

- Eating a wider variety of fruits, vegetables, nuts, legumes and whole grains to obtain all the nutrients needed and to support biodiversity.

- Buying local and seasonal, supporting products labelled 'organic', and 'Fairtrade'/'Rainforest Alliance'.

- When buying and eating meat, dairy, eggs and fish, think quality rather than quantity, cutting down on your weekly consumption. Choose produce directly from farms or fishermen, from butchers, fishmongers and supermarkets that follow/support regenerative and animal welfare farming and fishing practices. Here in Britain look for labels like 'free-range', 'grass fed', 'organic' 'non GM fed','MSC', 'Freedom Food – RSPCA monitored'.

- Cut down on eating too many refined carbohydrates, such as white bread, white rice, maize, and of course sugar.

- Bake your own cakes or biscuits, and have them as an occasional treat, rather than a daily food.

– Cut down on/avoid food and drink which is highly processed and high in additives and added sugars, like fizzy drinks, ready meals, sauces like ketchup, commercially baked goods, packaged snacks like cereal bars or crisps.

– Cook at home, sharing the task with all members of the family. Pass on food traditions and make up new ones, and enjoy the fruits of your labour around the kitchen table.

– Plan ahead, buy in bulk, cook in bulk, freeze meals or leftovers to be enjoyed at a later time. Besides saving work, you will also avoid waste.

– Share food, resources and knowledge with family and friends, with your community, with people in need.

Our choice of food will influence the demand on the food market and send clear signals all the way to the food producers and to governments.

The island centres of the Iona Community on Iona and Mull have for years been serving a mainly vegetarian diet, acknowledging the fact that the costs for the environment of industrial-style meat production are far higher than those of vegetables, fruit, nuts, seeds, beans and pulses.

We serve high-animal-welfare meat once or twice a week, and also fish, dairy and eggs, incorporating all into a varied, colourful, tasty, mainly vegetarian diet.

Living here, surrounded by farmland and the sea, we purchase our meat and fish, as much as possible, from local sources on Iona and Mull.

1. Yuval Noah Harari, *Sapiens – A Brief History of Humankind*, pages 13 & 14. Vintage, London.
2. Food and Agriculture Organisation of the United Nations (and others), *The State of Food Security and Nutrition in the World 2020*. Online publication: http://www.fao.org/3/ca9692en/online/ca9692en.html
3. EAT-Lancet Commission, *Brief For Everyone*. Online publication: https://eatforum.org/lancet-commission/eatinghealthyandsustainable/
4. Tim Spector, *The Diet Myth*. Weidenfeld & Nicolson, 2016, London.
5. EAT-Lancet Commission, *Food Planet Health*. Online publication: https://eatforum.org/content/uploads/2019/07/EAT-Lancet_Commission_Summary_Report.pdf

About the recipes

Some of the recipes have been created by me, some I inherited on smudged pieces of paper from former Abbey cooks, some are by friends or inspired by famous or not so famous chefs. I will credit the latter if that is the case.

The amounts of ingredients are given in metric measurements – grams, millilitres, litres etc, and, where appropriate, spoon measures. If you would like to convert an ingredients list to cup measures or the old imperial system, please use conversion tables which are freely available online.

I am quite pernickety in my explanations and sometimes you might be tempted to ignore some steps. While cooking is a creative process with lots of freedom to experiment, there are some rules which, if followed, do help to create not just edible food, but amazing dishes which 'shine' in their flavour and texture. Those seemingly little things like suggested cooking times, the way vegetables are chopped or how long to mix baking ingredients will often make a huge difference.

So here are some cooking tips which are close to my heart:

- It is advisable to read through the whole recipe before starting the cooking or baking process! Too many times I have seen some of my fellow enthusiastic volunteer cooks just putting all the ingredients from the list into the pot in one go.

- 'Bring to the boil, then cook for 5 minutes' – make sure you measure those 5 minutes from the point when food has started boiling (bubbling up). 'Bringing something to the boil' might take quite a while, depending on the power of the cooker. This is not part of the 'cooking time'. Also, covering your pot will always reduce the time it needs to come to the boil. And it saves energy.

- A lot of dishes improve with long, slow cooking, whether it's a tomato sauce, a lentil soup or a meat stew – so be patient and don't cut down on those hours of simmering …

On oven temperatures: All temperatures given are for electric static ovens, electric fan ovens and gas. These temperatures are a guideline – you will know your cooker best, so adjust if necessary.

On ingredients: A lot of the vegetables can be exchanged for others – so don't give up on Moroccan Tagine if you don't have butternut squash in the house, just use carrots instead. While some ingredients will always have to be imported (ginger, bananas) quite a few vegetables are now seasonally grown in the UK. For example, in mid/late summer you will find aubergines from British polytunnels, so look out for the country of origin on the packaging. Try to buy local and seasonal; for imported produce like cocoa, chocolate, coffee, bananas etc, source fairly traded goods. This way you support companies which pay their growers decent wages.

Gluten free/dairy free/vegan: I have marked foods GF (gluten free) and/or DF (dairy free) if the recipes do not contain these allergens. I have also indicated vegan recipes. However, remember to check the labels of any processed ingredients like mustard, soya sauce, mayonnaise etc to ensure that they don't contain allergens/animal products. Some recipes are labelled 'optionally' GF or DF – in this case ingredients can be easily exchanged to make them free of allergens.

On spices: For convenience we use ground spices at the Abbey. At home I like using whole ones – while they add a bit more work, they are more aromatic, as the ground stuff quickly loses its potency after opening. So if you have a spice mill or pestle and mortar, use it and grind freshly toasted spices for a deeper flavour.

On equipment

Today's kitchens are generally well equipped. Here is a list of tools I would sorely miss if I didn't have them in my home kitchen:

For cutting, pureeing and slicing:
- Knives. Very useful are:
- A large knife, with a broad blade that curves upwards towards the tip and allows a rocking movement for fine mincing
- A small vegetable knife
- A bread knife with a serrated edge
- A vegetable peeler

Keep your knives sharp (there are pull through sharpeners available if you struggle with a sharpening stone and steel) – injuries often happen if knives are blunt as one uses too much strength to compensate for bluntness.

- Mandoline grater and slicer
- A fine grater, e.g. microplane
- A kitchen processor (for pureeing, but also slicing, grating, etc)
- A stick soup blender (though the above will do but will take longer)
- A selection of chopping boards – colour-coded ones for different food groups are good

Preparation and cooking vessels:
- Heavy-based saucepans and frying pans
- Stainless steel, ceramic, glass and/or plastic bowls
- Baking and roasting trays
- Bread tins and cake tins

For mixing and food handling:
- Electric hand mixer or a Kenwood-style kitchen machine
- Two hand whisks, different sizes
- Two spatulas, different sizes
- Wooden spoons
- Large metal spoons/serving spoons
- Metal tongs

For measuring
- Electronic or mechanical scale
- Measuring spoons – these do not need to be bought in a speciality shop – just make sure you have the following three spoons in your drawer:
  - a teaspoon (tsp) which should hold 5 ml of liquid or powder
  - a dessertspoon which should hold 10 ml
  - a tablespoon (tbsp) which should hold 15 ml

On suppliers of ingredients

A list of more specialised ingredients and where you can find them:

Buckwheat groats/buckwheat flour: health food shop; you might find flour in larger supermarkets

Dried lime leaves: in the spice aisle of big supermarkets, Asian grocers

Fish sauce: large supermarkets, Asian grocers

Preserved lemons: large supermarkets, Middle Eastern grocers

Tahini (sesame paste): most big supermarkets, health food shops, Middle Eastern grocers

Tamari sauce (similar to soy sauce but gluten free): big supermarkets, wholefood shops, Asian grocers

We buy a lot of our dry ingredients at the Abbey from the Greencity Coop in Glasgow, an excellent supplier of wholefoods.

Personally, living on a small island far away from speciality shops, besides using Greencity, I purchase more unusual ingredients from online shops such as SousChef.co.uk which offer a great range of specialised food from near and far.

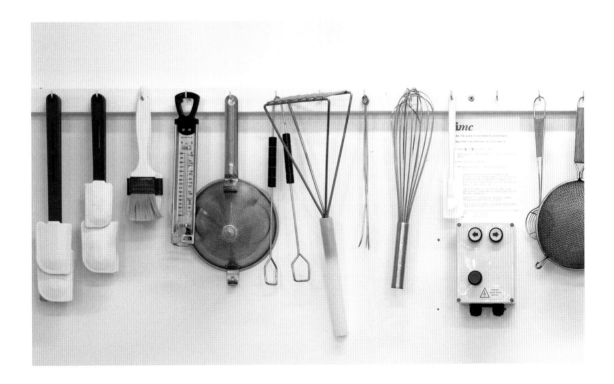

Breakfast!

After the sounding of the waking bell our guests will slowly gather in anticipation of the first cup of coffee or tea of the day. Breakfast is a simple affair, starting with a bowl of steaming porridge or cereal, and finishing with some home-made toast with fruity jam or marmalade.

Porridge

In my opinion, whether you want to eat your porridge sweet or plain/savoury, it needs to be made with salt. Just enough to bring out the flavour of the oats, not to make it taste salty.

We make our porridge in a double boiler to avoid having to employ a member of staff solely to stir the porridge for 30 minutes in the morning. (Using a normal pan and having the breakfast cook looking after it while making bread and scones resulted too often in a burnt pan and strange-tasting porridge!) For small portions at home, make it in a wee pan – you will not get the creamy texture most people love if you make it in the microwave.

2 portions:
1 cup porridge oats
2½-3 cups cold water
½ tsp salt

If you remember, soak the porridge in 2½ cups of water the evening before which isn't only convenient for the morning but also aids digestion, as the oats go through pre-fermentation overnight.

The following morning, bring it to boil on a medium heat, stirring most of the time. Once boiling, leave to cook on a low heat for a further two minutes, adding more water if you prefer your porridge more runny, then serve.

(Soak the porridge pan in cold water which makes it much easier to clean after breakfast.)

While there might be people who will eat their porridge just plain from the pot, most of us will add some 'sprinkles' …

I eat mine at home with a teaspoon each of tahini and ground linseeds, and diced fruit (berries, ripe pear, apple, banana) stirred through it. My husband loves a big blob of yoghurt and coconut 'milk' drink with his.

Cinnamon sugar was a great hit with most kitchen staff in the season of 2021 – we always had it pre-mixed (1:6 cinnamon to sugar) on the shelf.

Cream, fruit compotes, honey, you name it – there are barely any limits on how to enrich this simple nourishing fare.

And if there is some left over or forgotten – the latter happens often if one is in the middle of cooking – it's actually really good cold with a bit of jam on top!

Bread

The food that guests and staff alike comment on most is our homemade bread. Simple to make, just as long as you have a bit of time, and oh so rewarding to eat. For years now, it has been Andrew Whitley and his book *Bread Matters* which have inspired the bread-making process for both wheat and gluten free baking at the Abbey. Using good ingredients and giving them the time needed is the secret to a good loaf.

Basic wheat bread (2 loaves)

We use the sponge method, where some of the flour, yeast and some water are combined the day before to give the yeast time to ferment which helps develop flavour, nutrition content and digesti-bility of the bread. The sponge also has a beneficial effect on the structure of the final dough, resulting in strong gluten development which will hold a lot of air and produce large loaves. While we all love a soft white loaf, we tend to make a light wholemeal bread most days – it's more flavourful and healthy.

The day before you want to bake bread:

Into a bowl or plastic container (with lid) big enough for the contents to expand at least three times put:

> *2 level tsp dried yeast (we use Doves Farm)*
> *200 ml lukewarm water*
> *220 g wholemeal bread flour*

Mix with a spoon until well combined. Cover with a lid or plastic bag and leave up to 18 hours at room temperature to ferment.

The next day:

> *Overnight sponge (see above)*
> *450 g wholemeal bread flour*
> *200 g strong white flour*
> *2 slightly heaped tsp fine sea salt*
> *420-450 ml lukewarm water*
> *2 tbsp olive oil or sunflower oil*

Place sponge, flour and salt into a bowl (the bowl of the kitchen mixer if you use one for kneading). Add most of the water and mix with your hands (or your kitchen mixer, dough hook attached) into a rough dough. Add all water if needed, or more if the dough seems very dry. Remember that the flour will absorb more liquid while you are working the dough.

Kneading by hand: Turn out onto a clean kitchen surface, and work it for about 15 minutes until the dough starts to become silky and stretchy, and no longer sticks to the surface. Do not be tempted to add extra flour as this will make the bread too dry – if the dough is still sticky, the gluten is not fully developed, so keep on kneading for longer.

Add the oil – at first it will seem that dough and fat do not want to mix; however, work away patiently for another 3-5 minutes, and the mixture will come together.

By kitchen machine: Knead using the dough hook until the dough is silky and smooth. This will take about 8-10 minutes. Now add the oil. Knead for a further 2 minutes until well incorporated.

Cover with a tea towel and leave in a warm but not hot place to rise for 1 hour.

Grease two 900 g/2 lb loaf tins with oil.

After an hour, turn the risen dough onto a clean kitchen surface – a plastic scraper or spatula works well to scrape out most of it, which will make cleaning easier.

Divide the dough into two pieces, flatten each piece by stretching the dough out, then roll up into a sausage and place this into the tins – again, do not be tempted to add flour here. I tell the volunteers who come to cook with me: 'Be the boss of the dough!' – work swiftly so it doesn't stick too much on your hands and implements.

Sprinkle the dough lightly with flour (this will prevent the towel from sticking and also looks good) and cover with a tea towel. Leave the tins in a warm place for about 30-40 minutes or even longer (the shorter time for hot summer days or kitchens with a toasty range oven, the longer for cool draughty cottages) until the size of the dough has about doubled.

While the bread is rising, preheat your oven to 220 C (425 F) static/200 C (400 F) fan/gas 6-7 – this is really important, as bread needs to go into a hot oven.

Once appreciably grown in size, place the loaves into the oven and bake for 45 minutes.

After baking, turn out of the tin and leave to cool on a cooling rack.

Special breads and what to add:

Rosemary and rock salt: Use only strong white flour, and add 2 tsp dried or 3 tsp freshly chopped rosemary while making the final dough. Brush the top of the loaf with olive oil and sprinkle with rock salt before the final rise.

Sun-dried tomato and olive: At the same point as adding oil, add 3 tbsp stoned and drained olives (chopped or whole) and 2 tbsp sun-dried tomato (I prefer the dry ones rather than marinated in oil – the latter will most probably 'dissolve' during the kneading process, which still makes for a good bread, but it will lack the distinct pieces of tomato to bite into). Add only 1½ tsp salt.

White loaf with nigella seeds: Use only strong white flour and add 3 tsp nigella (aka black onion seeds) to the bread mix.

Treacle, fennel and coriander: Adapted from Andrew Whitley's Borodinsky bread (which is a rye sourdough loaf from Russia): mix 1 tbsp treacle or molasses into the water, and, at the same time as adding oil, add 2 tsp fennel and 2 tsp coriander seeds to your bread mix.

Multi-seed loaf: At the same time as adding oil, add ½ cup each of sunflower, sesame and pumpkin seeds to the bread. I suggest soaking the seeds in cold water for 15 minutes, then draining them thoroughly before adding – this will prevent the seeds absorbing too much water from the bread (which would dry it out).

Wholemeal and rye loaf: Change the flour content for making the final dough: use 250 g wholemeal flour, 200 g strong white flour and 200 g wholemeal rye flour. As rye absorbs more water, you will have to add more liquid.

Alma's porridge bread (wheat free)

Alma, a volunteer from Ireland, introduced me to this fantastic recipe – it's quickly made, no fermentation needed as it uses bicarbonate of soda as a raising agent. The treacle in it makes it very more-ish – a slice or two with some butter will leave you feeling quite satisfied.

> *500 ml buttermilk*
> *1 tsp black treacle*
> *1 egg*
> *400 g porridge oats*
> *2 tbsp seeds (sunflower, pumpkin, etc) – optional*
> *2 tsp bicarbonate of soda*
> *1 tsp salt*

Preheat your oven to 200 C (400 F) static/180 C (350 F) fan/gas 6. Grease a 900 g/2 lb loaf tin with oil.

Mix 500 ml buttermilk with treacle and egg, using a hand whisk. Measure the oats, seeds if using, bicarbonate of soda and salt into a bigger bowl. Stir through, before adding the liquid. Mix well, then turn into the prepared bread tin. Flatten and sprinkle with some more oats.

Bake in the oven for 30 minutes, then turn the heat down to 170 C (340 F) static/150 C (300 F) fan/gas 4, and continue baking for another 35 minutes.

Turn out of the tin and leave to cool on a cooling rack – wait at least 2 hours before slicing it.

Gluten free bread

With more people suffering from an intolerance to wheat or coeliac disease, baking gluten free bread has become quite normal here. In its taste and texture it's very different from wheat bread. Delicious when freshly baked, it dries out more quickly than wheat bread. However, it always makes great toast and is a good alternative if you have to avoid wheat.

I personally prefer using Doves Farm plain white flour (rather than their bread flours), which is a mix of rice, potato, tapioca, maize and buckwheat and has no additives such as xanthan gum added, keeping it as natural as possible.

> Makes 2 loaves in 900 g/2lb tins
> 100 g gluten free oats
> 20 g brown or golden linseeds
> 100 g sunflower or pumpkin seeds
> 350 ml hot water from the kettle
> 550 ml cold water (or 250 ml cold water and 300 ml cold milk, which will make the crumb softer)
> 600 g Doves Farm plain flour
> 200 g buckwheat flour (or more plain flour if not at hand)
> 3 heaped tsp easy-bake yeast
> 2 tbsp sunflower or olive oil
> 1 tbsp vinegar (we use apple cider vinegar)
> 2 tsp salt

Place oats, linseed and other chosen seeds into a big bowl, add the 350 ml hot water, stir and leave to soak for 10 minutes.

Now add cold water (or cold water and milk), flours, yeast, oil, vinegar and salt, and mix all thoroughly until well combined. The dough should be wet, like a thick batter or porridge, in its consistency – do not expect it to look and feel like wheat dough. Add more water if it seems hard to stir – different flours will absorb different amounts of liquid.

Grease two 900 g/2 lb loaf tins with oil, then scrape in the dough. Leave in a warm place for about 1 hour, until it has just about risen by ⅓. Try not to let it overproof, or it might collapse when you put it in the oven for baking.

Preheat your oven to 220 C (static)/200 C (fan)/gas mark 7, while the bread is rising.

Bake the loaves for 50 minutes, then leave to cool, out of their tins. You can start eating it when it's still slightly warm but try not to cut it when hot.

I suggest freezing one loaf – we often cut it up first, with a piece of baking parchment between each slice, and defrost it by the slice in a toaster.

Gluten free flatbread: You can bake this also as a flatbread. Instead of using bread tins, line two 25x30 cm baking trays with baking parchment, and scrape the mix on top, flattening it well. Leave to rise, then bake at 200 C for 23-25minutes until browned on top.

Sandwich Spreads

Hummus (GF/vegan)

Originating from the Middle East, this has been a lunchtime staple longer than I have been working here. It was Hanna, a cook from Bethlehem who came to volunteer in the Abbey kitchen, who showed me how to make good hummus and, for that matter, good falafel too (see recipe page 97). Hanna didn't give me amounts, he just felt and mixed and tasted and added – so here is what we still make today following his instructions.

You will need a food processor or liquidiser. This will make a large amount of hummus, enough for a big party, or to feed a family for the next three days ...

> *220 g dried chickpeas*
> *½ tsp bicarbonate of soda.*
> *½ tsp ground coriander*
> *juice of half a large lemon*
> *1 clove of garlic, crushed (use more if you want)*
> *1-1½ tsp fine sea salt*
> *½ cup cold water*
> *3 tbsp tahini*
> *3 tbsp olive oil, plus extra for serving*

Soak the chickpeas overnight in plenty of water – at least 700 ml. Add the bicarbonate of soda – this will help to soften the chickpeas. (You can also use tinned chickpeas – however, I find them often to be not soft enough, so I would cook them for another 10-20 minutes before making into hummus. You will need about 550 g of drained weight for this recipe.)

The next day, drain and wash the chickpeas, then place into a pan and cover with fresh cold water. Bring to a boil, skimming off any scum which will form in the first few minutes of boiling.

Keep the chickpeas boiling on a medium heat, refilling water if necessary. By the end of this process, the chickpeas should be very soft. You should be able to squash them easily between your fingers into a soft mush. This will take 40-50 minutes, though sometimes up to 1½ hours if the chickpeas are a bit old. Do not rush this process; smooth and creamy hummus can only be achieved with very soft chickpeas.

Drain the chickpeas and discard the cooking liquid (except if you want to use it to make vegan meringue – but that's for another cookbook!).

Place into a food processor together with lemon juice and half of the water, and blend until you have a smooth paste. Add crushed garlic, salt, coriander, and the rest of the water and process for a further minute. Add tahini, and continue whizzing for at least another 2 minutes to get a creamy, smooth texture. If it seems too stiff, add more water. I find that hummus made with still warm chickpeas will be stiffer once cooled, so you might want to make it on the runny side.

Scrape the mixture into a bowl or container, then stir through olive oil.

Serve with some more olive oil drizzled on top, sprinkled with some parsley, zaatar or sumac. It is really best when still slightly warm.

The hummus will keep well for three days in the fridge, but always let it come back to room temperature before serving.

Egg mayonnaise (GF, DF)

Especially delicious when made with fresh farm eggs – this is just a delight on fresh crusty bread.

Serves 4
4 eggs
1 heaped tbsp mayonnaise
1 level tsp wholegrain mustard (needs to be GF)
½ tsp salt
½ tsp freshly ground pepper
1 tbsp freshly chopped chives

Place the eggs into a pan and cover with cold water. Cover with a lid and bring to the boil. Once boiling, set your timer for 6 minutes – this should achieve eggs which are almost hard-boiled but with a slightly soft centre.

Drain the eggs and leave them under running cold water for 20 seconds.

Peel eggs, chop roughly and place into a bowl with mayonnaise, mustard, salt and pepper. Using a fork, squish and mix to your preferred consistency. Taste and adjust if necessary. Serve sprinkled with chives.

Soup

Having cooked, served and eaten hundreds of bowls of soup during my time at the Abbey, I never tire of it. It seems like the perfect food: warm, with ever-changing tastes and textures, very portable (in a soup flask), healthy and quick to make. The following is a small selection of the quite huge Abbey repertoire. They make big pans of soup for a large family – if it's too much for you, just freeze in portions.

Carrot, orange and coriander soup

Bright and zesty, this soup is uplifting. Perfect for those dreich (good Scottish word!) winter days.

> *1 large onion, chopped*
> *1 clove of garlic, minced*
> *1 level tsp ground coriander*
> *6 large carrots, peeled and chopped*
> *1 small potato, scrubbed and diced*
> *Zest and juice of one orange (washed under warm water)*
> *1.2 ltr vegetable stock*
> *Freshly ground pepper and salt*

Fry the onion in some sunflower oil until transparent. Add garlic and sweat for another minute before adding carrots, coriander, potato, orange zest and juice and the vegetable stock. Cover with a lid and bring the soup to a boil on high heat. Once bubbling, turn it down to a simmer and cook for 30-40 minutes until the carrots are soft.

Blend to a smooth soup, and add freshly ground pepper and salt to taste.

Celeriac and potato soup (GF/VEGAN)

This is very much an adaptation of a Saxon Kartoffelsuppe, potato soup, which back in Germany is often served with a delicious smooth smoked pork sausage. I have changed the balance towards the celeriac, making it lighter than the original.

> Serves 4-6
> *1 medium onion, chopped*
> *Sunflower oil*
> *1 medium celeriac, about 10-12 cm in diameter, peeled and diced*
> *2 medium-sized potatoes, scrubbed and diced*
> *1 medium-sized carrot, peeled and sliced*
> *1.2 ltr vegetable stock*
> *Lemon juice, salt and pepper*
> *Fresh parsley or lovage to serve*

Fry the onion on a medium heat in sunflower oil until transparent, then add the vegetables, sweating them for 5 minutes, stirring frequently. Now add the vegetable stock, cover the pan with a lid and bring the soup to a boil. Once boiling, simmer on a low heat, covered, for 30-40 minutes until vegetables are all soft.

Using a stick blender or a kitchen processor, blend to a very smooth consistency. If too thick, add more water at this stage.

Season with ½ tsp freshly ground pepper and 1 tsp lemon juice, stir well, taste and adjust if necessary. Serve with a generous topping of chopped parsley or lovage.

Variation: Celeriac and blue cheese soup

After making the soup following the above recipe, stir in 150 ml cream, then crumble in 100 g strong-tasting blue cheese such as Gorgonzola or Stilton and stir through until melted. Warm up again if necessary and serve.

Beetroot, sweet potato and ginger soup

Extraordinary in its colour and vibrant in taste, this soup is one of my personal favourites. I make it a lot in summer and autumn, when fresh garden beetroot are plentiful, but if they are not available, the vacuum-packed beets sold all year round will do too.

Do not peel the sweet potato – most of its nutritional goodness lies in and just below the peel. Just make sure to blend the soup until very smooth to avoid any unpleasant 'bits'.

> Serves 6
> *1 medium onion, chopped*
> *2 cloves of garlic, minced*
> *Sunflower oil*
> *A chunky, thumb-length piece of ginger*
> *1 large, fist-sized (or two or three smaller) beetroot, peeled and diced*
> *1 large, about 700 g, sweet potato, scrubbed and diced*
> *1.2 ltr vegetable stock*
> *Salt and pepper*
> *1 dessertspoon lemon juice*

Fry onion and garlic gently on a low heat in some sunflower oil until transparent.

Wash the ginger, then grate finely, including the peel.

Add the beetroot and sweet potatoes to the fried onions and continue frying gently for a further 5 minutes. Now add the vegetable stock, cover with a lid and bring to a boil on a high heat. Once boiling, turn down to a simmer and cook for 30-40 minutes until the beets are soft.

Add ½ tsp salt and lemon juice, then blend to a smooth consistency. Add ½ tsp pepper, stir well, taste and adjust seasoning if necessary.

Serve with a good blob of natural yoghurt.

Sweetcorn chowder (GF)

While the word 'chowder' reminds most of us of a creamy, rich, seafood soup, this mild vegetarian version is just as tasty!

Serves 6

1 medium onion, chopped
1 tbsp butter or sunflower oil
1 clove of garlic, minced
3 medium-sized potatoes, washed and diced
4 large sticks of celery, washed and sliced
400 g of sweetcorn, frozen or tinned, drained weight
1.2 ltr vegetable stock
Bay leaf
60 ml double cream
Nutmeg, salt, freshly ground pepper, lemon juice, fresh parsley

Fry onions in butter or oil until transparent, but not browned. Add garlic, celery, potatoes and sweetcorn and sweat for 1 minute. Add the vegetable stock and the bay leaf, cover and bring to the boil.

Simmer on a low heat for 30-40 minutes until all the vegetables are soft. Fish out the bay leaf and discard. Using a jug, scoop out half of the vegetables, putting them aside.

Blend the rest of the soup in the pan to a smooth consistency using a stick blender or food processor. Stir in the chunky reserved vegetables, add ½ tsp ground nutmeg, 1 tsp lemon juice, the cream, 2 tbsp of freshly chopped parsley, and freshly ground pepper and salt to taste.

Cauliflower and Cheddar cheese soup (GF)

Comforting and smooth – this has been an Abbey favourite since the first time we served it.

Serves 6
1 tbsp sunflower oil
1 medium onion, chopped
1 large cauliflower, washed and chopped, including the tender stem
2 medium-sized floury potatoes, washed and diced
1.2 ltr vegetable stock
Freshly ground pepper, salt
½ tsp freshly grated nutmeg
50 ml cream
80 g mature Cheddar, grated
1-2 tsp lemon juice

Fry the onion gently, without browning, in some sunflower oil. Add diced potatoes and vegetable stock, bring to boil, cover and simmer for 15 minutes.

The potatoes should now be soft. Add cauliflower. (Don't be tempted to add more water at this stage even if the vegetables are not submerged in the stock – cauliflower contains a lot of water so adding more stock at this point would result in a thin soup.) Bring to the boil again. Cook for a further 8-12 minutes until the cauliflower is just tender.

Blend to a very smooth soup. Add cream and grated nutmeg, mix well, then stir in the cheese. Add lemon juice, some salt and freshly ground pepper to taste. Adjust if necessary.

If you wish to keep this soup vegan, omit cream and cheese, and add 80 ml of a cream alternative (e.g. oat cream) instead.

Tomato soup with smoked paprika (GF/VEGAN)

If you have a glut of tomatoes from your own polytunnel or greenhouse, make this soup with fresh (peeled) tomatoes. However, I find it is just as good if you use tins of good quality Italian chopped tomatoes.

The secret of anything with tomato as a base is the cooking time – simmer it for as long as possible, to give time for the flavours to mingle and the acidity of the tomatoes to mellow.

Serves 6
1 tbsp olive oil
1 medium onion, chopped
2 cloves of garlic, minced
3 sticks of celery, washed and sliced
2 medium-sized carrots, scrubbed or peeled, sliced
1 small potato, a bit bigger than a golf ball, scrubbed and diced
1 x 400 g tin chopped tomatoes
2 heaped tbsp tomato puree
½ tsp soft brown sugar
800 ml water
1 vegetable stock cube or 1 heaped tsp vegetable stock powder
1 tsp smoked paprika
Pepper and salt
Freshly chopped basil to serve

Fry onions in olive oil until transparent, then add all other vegetables.

Sweat for 5 minutes, stirring frequently, on medium heat, then add chopped tomatoes and tomato puree, water (rinse out the tin with it), vegetable stock cube, sugar and smoked paprika.

Cover the pan, bring to the boil on a high heat, then turn to low. Leave simmering, with a lid on, for at least 1 hour, though 2 hours is better. Check it every 30 min to make sure it doesn't get too thick and starts sticking to the bottom of the pan – if that is so, add some more water.

Blend the soup until very smooth. Add ½ tsp of salt and pepper, taste and adjust if necessary.

Serve drizzled with olive oil, and some balsamic vinegar if at hand

Swede (turnip) and leek soup (GF, VEGAN)

This soup might surprise you with its sweet, warming flavours, not at all 'cabbagey' or boring, a quality often attributed to the good old swede (turnip/rutabaga).

Take your time when chopping the vegetables (as finely as possible) and sweating the swede – both will help immensely in making this soup a success.

> Serves 4-6
> 1 tbsp sunflower oil
> 1 small swede/turnip – peeled weight about 500 g – diced as finely as possible
> 1 small onion, finely chopped
> 1 medium-sized leek, washed well, halved lengthwise and thinly sliced
> 2 small potatoes, scrubbed and very finely diced
> 1½ tsp of cumin seeds
> ½ tsp turmeric
> 1 bay leaf
> 1 ltr vegetable stock
> Pepper and salt

Heat up a heavy-based pan, and add the sunflower oil and finely diced swede/turnip. Heat up until it starts sizzling – now turn down to a low heat, put a lid on the pan and sweat the swede for 10-15 minutes until orange and very soft. Give it all a stir every 5 minutes and adjust the heat during the cooking process – the swede should not fry in the oil, or boil in its own liquid, but just steam in its evaporating juices.

When done, increase heat to medium and add onions and leeks and stir-fry until just wilted.

Add spices, bay leaf and vegetable stock, and bring the soup, covered with a lid, to a boil. Once boiling, turn down to a simmer, and cook for 10 minutes.

Add ½ tsp salt or more to taste and season richly with grated pepper. Serve with some freshly chopped parsley if at hand.

Green goddess soup (GF, VEGAN)

This soup was first made by my fellow volunteer Elizabeth when we worked together in the Iona Community's Coffee House in 1999. We called it 'Green Goddess soup', looking for a more exciting title than 'Leek, courgette and lentil'.

> Serves 6
> 1 tbsp olive oil
> 1 medium onion, chopped
> 3 courgettes (about 20 cm long), washed and sliced

1 large, chunky leek, washed and sliced
1 clove of garlic, chopped
150 g red lentils
1 tsp cumin
1 tsp basil
1.2 ltr vegetable stock
Pepper and salt
1 dessertspoon lemon juice

Fry the onion gently in olive oil until transparent, then add other vegetables and garlic. Stir-fry for 5 minutes without browning.

Add cumin and basil, red lentils and the vegetable stock. Cover and bring to boil, stirring from time to time.

Once boiling, turn heat down to medium and leave to simmer for 20 minutes. Stir occasionally.

Blend to a smooth soup, adding more water if it seems too thick. Season with pepper and salt and lemon juice to taste.

Thai style leek and sweet potato soup (GF, VEGAN)

Leek and potato soup must be, beside lentil, the most served and loved soup in Britain. It always surprises me how so few ingredients (leek, potato and good stock) make such a beautiful soup with a deep flavour.

This is my take on the trusted favourite, Thai style, adding warming spices and coconut milk, and replacing potatoes with sweet potatoes.

Serves 6
1 tbsp sunflower oil
2 large leeks, washed well, halved lengthways and sliced finely
2 cloves of garlic, minced
1 large sweet potato (about 600 g unpeeled weight), peeled and diced
1 level tsp turmeric
A 2-cm-long chunky piece of ginger
½ tsp of chilli flakes or 1 tsp freshly chopped chilli (adapt to how hot you like it!)
2 tsp ground coriander
6 cm piece of ginger, peeled and grated (or 1 heaped tsp ground ginger)
½ tsp brown sugar
4 lime leaves (or the zest of one well-washed lime)
1 ltr vegetable stock
400 ml tin of coconut milk
1 tbsp lime juice (or lemon juice)
Freshly chopped coriander to serve

Warm up sunflower oil in a pan and stir-fry the leeks and garlic until wilted.

Add sweet potatoes, sugar, lime leaves, grated ginger and spices, then the vegetable stock.

Cover with a lid, bring to the boil. Once boiling, leave to simmer for 25 min over a low heat.

After the cooking time, fish out the lime leaves, and add the coconut milk and lime juice. Season with salt and pepper to taste. Warm through and serve with a generous sprinkling of freshly chopped coriander.

Courgette, carrot and chilli soup (GF, VEGAN)

A very light and flavourful soup – it came to the island when the local primary school had a 6-week 'Soup-a-box' scheme going. Islanders could sign up to receive a recipe and ingredients for a soup once a week. Boxes were delivered on foot or bike by the pupils. The project was very successful, with some good funds raised for the 'school coffers', and new recipes introduced into homes.

> Serves 4-6
> 1 medium onion, chopped
> 1 clove of garlic, minced
> Sunflower oil
> 4 large carrots, scrubbed or peeled, sliced
> 2 large courgettes (about 20-25 cm long), washed and sliced
> 1-1.2 ltr vegetable stock
> Salt and pepper
> 1 dessertspoon lemon juice
> Freshly chopped red chilli, 1 tsp or more (or ½ tsp chili flakes)

Fry the onion in some sunflower oil until transparent, then add the garlic, carrots and courgettes, and sweat, stirring occasionally, for 5 minutes on a medium heat.

Add 1 ltr of the vegetable stock, cover with a lid and bring to boil.

Once boiling, turn heat down to a simmer, and cook for 30 minutes.

Using a soup blender, puree to a smooth consistency, adding more stock to get a thick but runny soup.

Stir in as much chopped chilli (or chilli flakes) as you like, add lemon juice, and salt and pepper to taste.

Curried greens and split pea soup (GF, VEGAN)

A winter warmer – this thick and chunky soup is a meal in itself! We love serving it at the local 'Guy Fawkes' firework night – people all wrapped up, gathered in the fire station, hands cupped around beakers of hot steaming soup, watching the spectacle in the night sky.

It is an enriched dahl really so, as well as a soup, you can also serve this with rice or naan and a side salad as a nourishing main meal.

Serves 6
250 g yellow split peas, soaked overnight in plenty of water
  with ½ tsp bicarb of soda (which helps the pulses soften)
1 medium onion, finely chopped
2 cloves of garlic, minced
2 tsp medium curry powder (we use mild Madras)
1 tsp cumin seeds
½ tsp turmeric
150 g brown or green lentils
2 ltr vegetable stock
2 handfuls of finely chopped leafy greens, such as chard, spinach or kale
½ small broccoli, washed and cut into very small florets
½ tsp brown sugar
1 dessertspoon lemon juice
Salt and pepper

Sauté onions and garlic on a medium heat in some sunflower oil until transparent, then add spices and stir-fry for a further minute without browning.

Add drained split peas, lentils, the vegetable stock and sugar.

Cover the pan, bring to boil, then turn down to a simmer and cook for 45 minutes or longer until the split peas are starting to fall apart and the lentils are very soft. Stir regularly (if it gets badly stuck on the bottom, transfer to a new pan rather than stirring up burned bits into the beautifully bright yellow soup).

While the broth is cooking, cut up the broccoli into very small florets, and chop the greens finely.

When the split peas are soft and the soup has thickened, add broccoli and greens, cook for a further 5 minutes until the broccoli is just tender, then add lemon juice and salt and pepper to taste. Serve with a dollop of natural yoghurt and chopped coriander, and some chilli flakes if you like it hot.

Puy lentil and thyme soup (GF, VEGAN)

Another soup inspired by my German heritage – the addition of sugar and vinegar to a green lentil soup is very much a culinary characteristic of my region of Germany.

Serves 4-6
1 medium onion, finely chopped
2 cloves of garlic, minced
2 sticks of celery, washed and finely diced
½ small turnip, peeled and finely diced
1 large carrot, peeled or scrubbed, and finely diced
1 medium potato, scrubbed and finely diced
½ leek, finely sliced
180 g puy lentils (or green or brown lentils)
1.2 ltr vegetable stock
1 tsp ground cumin
1 tsp thyme
1 bay leaf
Pepper and salt
1 dessertspoon apple cider vinegar or white wine vinegar
½ tsp soft brown sugar

Fry onions in some sunflower oil until transparent, then add garlic and the vegetables and fry a bit longer until fragrant but not browned. Now add cumin, thyme, lentils, vegetable stock and bay leaf.

Cover, bring to the boil, simmer for 40 minutes or until lentils are soft. Add more water if too thick. Season with pepper and salt, add vinegar and sugar. Remove bay leaf, taste and adjust if necessary.

Salads

Celeriac and wholegrain mustard slaw (GF, optionally DF)

It is called, and may I say unjustly so, 'the ugly one' on the wooden boxes in which it gets delivered to the Abbey kitchen. It might look a bit alien, this knobbly vegetable, but its taste and texture are sensational: lighter in taste than celery, with a buttery crunch, it's excellent in salads and other dishes.

It browns quickly if exposed too long to the air, so keep in a bowl of water mixed with some vinegar if you don't use it immediately after peeling.

Optionally you could add a grated apple to this salad which will give it a pleasing fruity note, or a grated carrot, for an earthy sweet crunch – in both cases slightly reduce the amount of celeriac.

Serves 4-6
¼ of a large celeriac, peeled weight about 250 g
Dressing:
1½ heaped tsp wholegrain mustard
1 tbsp mayonnaise
1 tbsp natural or Greek style yoghurt (replace with DF yoghurt or more mayonnaise if you would like to keep the salad dairy free)
1 dessertspoon lemon juice
1 dessertspoon olive oil
1 tbsp freshly chopped parsley
½ tsp salt
½ tsp soft brown sugar
½ tsp freshly ground pepper

First prepare the dressing by mixing all the ingredients in a salad bowl with a hand whisk until well combined.

Grate the celeriac into julienne strips with a mandoline, or use the bigger holes of a box grater to shred it into fairly coarse bits.

Add to the dressing, stir well, then leave to mature for 30 minutes before serving.

Russian vegetable salad (GF, VEGAN)

A feast for eyes and taste buds – a good side salad for a BBQ, but also lovely with an omelette or a pan-fried piece of fish.

Serves 4-6
1 fist-sized fresh beetroot, scrubbed (or 3 small vacuum packed ones –
  omit the cooking process if using these)
6 small salad potatoes, washed
2 large carrots
200 g frozen peas (or fresh, if they are in season)
4 gherkins, finely sliced (use more if you have the tiny cornichon variety)
3 spring onions, washed and finely sliced

Dressing:
1 tbsp fresh dill, washed and chopped (or 1 tsp dried dill)
2 tbsp apple cider vinegar or wine vinegar
1 heaped tsp Dijon mustard (check your brand for wheat content)
1 tsp sugar
½-1 level tsp of salt
Pepper to taste
6 tbsp sunflower oil

First prepare the vegetables: Place the beetroot into a small pan, add water to cover it, put on a lid, and bring to boil, then continue cooking for 20-30 minutes until the beet is soft.

Chop the potatoes and carrots finely into 1 cm dice, then boil those and the peas in separate pans until soft – the peas will only need 1 minute boiling; carrots and potatoes should be soft but with bite after 5 minutes of cooking. Drain the vegetables, put aside to cool.

Make up the dressing by mixing all the ingredients in a bowl with a whisk.

When the beet is cool enough to handle, take off the peel – often it just slides off when pushed. Cut into 1 cm dice, then add ⅓ of the dressing and stir through.

Place cooled carrots, potatoes, peas, gherkins and spring onions into the bowl containing the rest of the dressing and gently mix.

Just before serving, add the beetroot into the bowl with the other vegetables and combine – if you do it too early the beetroot will dye all the other vegetables pink!

Cucumber salad with yoghurt and garlic dressing (GF)

This salad is adapted from a Greek dip/sauce called Tzatziki which you will also find under different names all over the Middle East. It goes extremely well with lamb meatballs or roast lamb, the clean taste of the yoghurt balancing the heavy, fatty meat, but it is also delicious with falafel.

Serves 4
The salad:
1 cucumber, washed

Dressing:
200 g natural or plain Greek-style yoghurt
1 small clove of garlic, very finely minced
1 tbsp olive oil
½ tsp caster sugar
1 tsp vinegar or lemon juice
½ tsp salt
½ tsp cracked pepper
Finely chopped mint to serve

Cut the cucumber into 1 cm dice, place them into a colander and sprinkle with salt to extract moisture and intensify the taste – leave for 15 minutes. Wash under cold water and leave to drain. Lay out on a serving platter or put into a salad bowl.

Mix the dressing in a separate bowl, then spoon onto the cucumber. Sprinkle with finely chopped mint.

Tzatziki (to serve as a dip with meat or falafel)
Grate only half of the washed (not peeled) cucumber roughly, place into a sieve, sprinkle with ½ tsp salt and leave to drain for 15 minutes. Mix the above dressing but do not add any more salt, then combine with the cucumber. Leave for at least an hour to mature.

Carrot and seed salad (GF, VEGAN)

One of my favourite salads (I think the carrot would be my desert island vegetable): there is crunch, there is nutty flavour, there is a good balance between sweet, sour and salty. And it still tastes good the next day.

Serves 4
Dressing:
1 tsp runny honey (to melt set honey, gently warm up in a wee saucepan
*   or in the microwave), or maple syrup*
Juice of ½ large lemon

1 tbsp toasted sesame oil
1 tsp tamari sauce (or soy sauce, which is not gluten free!)

The salad:
3 large carrots, peeled
3 tbsp sunflower seeds
1 tbsp sesame seeds

Mix the dressing in a salad bowl by putting in all ingredients and whisking together.

Place the seeds into a small saucepan and put over a medium heat. Stir most of the time, browning the seeds gently. Leave to cool.

Grate the carrots roughly and place into the bowl with the dressing. Stir through to coat all carrots, then sprinkle seeds on top of the salad and serve.

Kidney bean, sweetcorn and pepper salad (GF, VEGAN)

I remember eating this salad for the first time in 1990 when visiting my pen pal in West Germany. While there was always plenty to eat in East Germany, there certainly wasn't a huge variety of ingredients to be had. Fresh peppers were rarely for sale, sweetcorn grew widely but was mostly used for animal feed, and we had not heard of kidney beans before. So this simple salad was quite a revelation for me – the mixture of textures, colours, tastes just hit the spot.

Serves 6

120 g dried kidney beans, soaked overnight in plenty of water
   with ½ tsp bicarbonate of soda, which helps the beans to soften,
   or 1 x 400 g tin of kidney beans, drained
1 x 340 g tin of sweetcorn, drained
1 green and 1 red pepper

Dressing:
2½ tbsp olive oil
2 tbsp apple cider or white wine vinegar
½ tsp caster sugar
½ tsp salt
½ tsp freshly ground pepper

If using dried kidney beans:

After soaking them overnight, drain off the liquid, wash the beans, put into a pan and cover with fresh cold water. Bring to the boil, covered with a lid. Once boiling, turn heat down to medium and leave to cook for 20 minutes – after that, test for softness. You want beans that are beautifully floury, with no bite left. (Adding acid will harden the proteins in the beans, so once they get mixed with dressing, they will firm up a bit. Therefore it's not a bad idea to slightly overcook the beans.) Continue cooking if necessary, topping up the water level if required. Once the beans are soft, drain and leave to cool fully before mixing with the other ingredients.

If using tinned beans:

Have a taste. If they are crunchy/grainy, you could boil them for 10-15 minutes to make them softer – it will really improve the end result of the salad.

Wash the peppers thoroughly, cut in halves, remove the seeds, then chop into small dice.

Mix the dressing in a large salad bowl, then add peppers, drained sweetcorn and beans. Stir well. Leave to mature for 30 minutes, then taste and add more vinegar and salt if needed.

Serve sprinkled with some parsley if at hand.

Fennel and orange salad (GF, VEGAN)

Its aniseed flavour does put some people off eating fennel – however, the bulb is very mild-tasting and a lot of those who have reluctantly tried it in salads or stews actually find it quite tasty. Try it!

Serves 6-8
1 large fennel bulb, or two smaller ones
2 small oranges
Chopped fresh chilli, or a good pinch of chilli flakes
3 tbsp fresh chopped parsley

Dressing:
3 tbsp olive oil
2 tbsp lemon juice
½ tsp honey
A good pinch of salt

Make up the dressing by putting all ingredients into a jam jar, closing it and giving it a good shake.

Wash the fennel, then cut off most of the tough stalks. I find that the first layer around a bulb can be less tender, so take it off and keep it to put into your next soup or stew (e.g. tomato or celeriac soup).

Slice a thin layer off the bottom and discard.

Now cut the bulb in halves, then quarters, and slice each quarter thinly. Use a mandoline grater here which will make the job much easier. Lay out the fennel on a serving platter or put into a salad bowl.

Peel the orange and separate out the segments (or just dice it). Scatter these over the fennel.

Just before serving, shake the dressing again, then drizzle over the salad. Sprinkle richly with parsley and the chilli.

Waldorf salad (GF, optionally VEGAN)

An old classic, much loved here at the Abbey.

We often omit both yoghurt and walnuts – which makes it not only more allergy-friendly but, in my opinion, a better fit with some of our meals, like egg fried rice, smoked mackerel kedgeree or baked potatoes with homemade baked beans.

> Serves 4
> *3 large sticks of celery, or more if using the more tender heart, washed*
> *1 large dessert apple, washed*
> *A good bunch of parsley – a minimum of about 3 heaped tbsp when chopped*
> *Juice of one small lemon*
> *1 tbsp olive oil*
> *½ tsp caster sugar*
> *A good pinch of salt*
> *2 tbsp sultanas or raisins*
>
> *Optional:*
> *1 handful shelled walnuts*
> *2 tbsp Greek-style plain yoghurt or dairy free alternative*

Core and dice the apple finely, then place into a bowl and add the lemon juice immediately, stirring the fruit to coat it with the juice – this will prevent it from turning brown. Slice the celery and add to the bowl too.

Chop the parsley, stalks and all (the stalks contain a lot of the flavour, so chop them finely with a sharp knife), and add to the bowl along with all the other ingredients, including the yoghurt if using. This salad tastes best when freshly made, so stir through, optionally sprinkle with walnuts, and serve right away.

Crunchy Vietnamese-style salad (GF, VEGAN)

When in Glasgow, my family and I love going to the Hanoi Bike Shop, a restaurant in the city's West End. The freshly prepared food is always exciting, colourful and bursting with flavours. This salad was inspired by a visit there. The recipe makes a big hearty bowl.

Serves 4-6

1 large carrot, peeled
¼ of a small sweetheart cabbage or the heart of a small Savoy cabbage
1 red pepper, washed
½ cucumber, washed
A handful of fresh coriander and mint
2 spring onions, limp leaves trimmed off
3 tbsp unsalted roasted peanuts, crushed lightly with a pestle and mortar

Dressing:
3 tbsp lime juice
2-3 tsp soft brown sugar
1 tbsp fish sauce (there is vegan fish sauce available now)
2 tbsp sunflower oil
A good pinch of chilli flakes or some freshly chopped chilli
A small clove of garlic, very finely minced or pressed

First prepare the vegetables: Grate the carrot and cucumber roughly – a mandoline grater works well. Slice the cabbage and red pepper finely. Chop the herbs roughly. Slice the spring onions very finely, preferably diagonally. Place all into a salad bowl

Make the dressing by putting all the ingredients into a jam jar with lid, closing it and giving it a good shake.

Just before serving, dress the salad and toss well. (You might not need all of the dressing – the rest keeps in the fridge for 2 weeks and is rather good as a dipping sauce for spring rolls too.) Scatter peanuts on top and serve.

Simple cabbage salad

The humble cabbage! Not only tasty and nutritious, it's also one of those veg which keep for a long time – perfect for long winters in the North. We always have one kind in our fridge – whether for a traditional coleslaw, an addition to a stir-fry, or, at home, for making sauerkraut.

For this simple recipe, Dutch white, red, Savoy or sweetheart varieties are all good to use – the secret of the recipe is in the pounding of the cabbage!

> Serves 4
> ½ small cabbage – about 400 g
> 1 tbsp olive oil
> 1 dessertspoon apple cider vinegar
> ½ tsp salt
> A large pinch of brown sugar

I prefer using the fine setting of a mandoline grater for chopping up the cabbage, but a sharp knife and careful thin slicing will do just as well.

Place into a metal or strong plastic bowl (not glass or ceramic). Using the end of a rolling pin (the kind that is made of one piece of wood or synthetic material) pound the cabbage for half a minute or so, in order to soften it – white or red cabbage will need longer than a sweetheart variety, which is much more tender to start with. If a rolling pin is not available, you could also just 'massage' it with your hands. This will release flavour and some of the vegetable juice and make the cabbage easier to digest without losing too much of its crunch.

Make up the dressing in a separate bowl, then stir through.

> Optional extras:
> 1 tsp of toasted cumin or caraway seeds
> 2 tbsp toasted pumpkin seeds
> With red cabbage: a handful of toasted walnuts and 2-3 satsumas, diced

Tomato salsa (GF, VEGAN)

Although this is theoretically more a sauce than a salad, I will nevertheless include it in this chapter. After all, you could make it more salad-like by cutting the tomatoes into wedges instead of very small pieces.

This will have the best flavour if you make it when tomatoes are in season. Those you buy in the winter months in Britain are just not tasty enough. Instead, make a sauce with tinned tomatoes to go as a side.

Serves 4-6
A small clove of garlic, or ½ a big one
Juice of ½ lime
1 tbsp olive oil
½ tsp soft brown sugar
½ tsp salt
500 g tomatoes
2 spring onions
Fresh chilli or chilli flakes
2 tbsp roughly chopped coriander

Mince the half clove of garlic finely and place into a salad bowl. Add sugar, salt, lime juice, olive oil and as much or as little chilli as you like. Stir well.

Wash the tomatoes and spring onions, then chop them as finely as you can.

Chop the coriander – using both leaves and the tender stems.

If you are going to use the salsa in the next half hour, mix all ingredients together now. If not, put tomatoes, spring onions and coriander into a different container and mix just before serving. (The salt in the dressing draws out moisture from the tomatoes and will make the salsa watery if mixed too early.)

Honey and mustard dressing (GF, VEGAN)

Delicious on leafy salads. In summer when the garden produces an abundance of lettuce I always have a wee bottle prepared on the counter.

The following recipe makes plenty to last for a week.

> *100 ml the best extra virgin olive oil you can afford*
> *50 ml apple cider vinegar or lemon juice or other vinegar*
> *1 tsp runny honey (use 1 tsp brown sugar if you cannot have honey)*
> *1 tsp Dijon or wholegrain mustard*

Place all ingredients into a jar (with a well fitting lid) or bottle (using a funnel). Close the lid and shake until all ingredients have emulsified into a smooth liquid.

Tahini dressing (GF, VEGAN)

Another versatile dressing, originating in the Middle East, where sesame paste is used abundantly in cooking. Try it on roast vegetables, on fresh mixed salads or as a dip for falafel or vegetable sticks and pieces of pitta.

Best made in a jug-style kitchen processor, although you can make it by hand, mincing the garlic finely and mixing it all using a hand whisk.

> *1 clove of garlic*
> *45 g tahini paste*
> *65 ml lemon juice*
> *90 ml cold water*
> *½ tsp caster sugar*
> *A good pinch each of salt, pepper and allspice*
> *50 ml olive oil*

Place all ingredients into the bowl of a processor. Whiz to a smooth consistency. The dressing will keep for up to a week in the fridge in a closed container.

Gado gado dressing

Gado gado is an Indonesian salad of boiled eggs and potatoes, and a variety of other fresh or blanched vegetables, richly drizzled with a warm peanut dressing. While it can be served as a side, its hearty ingredients make this salad a substantial and tasty main course. Some people add fried tempeh or tofu to the selection for more texture and taste. Also, don't forget to serve prawn crackers on the side!

Being similar to a pad thai sauce, this dressing can also be mixed into a stir-fry of vegetables and noodles. Or served with roast vegetables and rice as another filling and tasty main course option. This recipe makes plenty, so any leftovers can be frozen and used for another dish.

> *1 clove of garlic*
> *2 shallots or a small onion – finely chopped*
> *Sunflower oil*
> *2 tsp soft brown sugar*
> *200 ml water*
> *150 g peanut butter*
> *200 ml coconut milk*
> *1 thumb-sized piece of ginger – finely grated*
> *Juice of 1-2 limes*
> *1 tbsp tamari sauce*
> *4 tsp fish sauce (or vegan 'fish sauce') – you can also replace it with extra tamari*
> *Freshly chopped chilli – as much or as little as you like …*

Gently fry the garlic and shallots in some sunflower oil until transparent but not browned. This should take 5 minutes.

Add ginger, sugar, water and coconut milk and heat up slowly. Put in the peanut butter and let it dissolve while stirring all the time. Don't worry if it seems a bit lumpy – when almost boiling, take off the heat and whizz to a smooth consistency with a soup blender, or in a kitchen processor. If it seems too thick (you want the consistency of custard), add some more water at this stage.

Season with the lime juice, tamari sauce and fish sauce if using; stir in the freshly chopped chilli. Use straight away, or leave to cool and store for up to three days in the fridge. Reheat gently to serve warm.

Vegetarian Main Courses

We love preparing vegetarian and vegan food using a rich and colourful variety of vegetables, fruits, beans, pulses, grains, nuts, seeds, eggs and cheeses. The world's recipe books are full of naturally tasty meat- and fish-free recipes and exploring these has been a great adventure over the years. Some recipes have come with volunteers from abroad, others have been found on holidays or been 'invented' in my kitchen.

Guests at the Abbey who arrive as staunch meat-eaters often comment on how much they have enjoyed the surprising variety of vegetarian food, and that they did not miss having meat every day.

Basic tomato sauce (GF, VEGAN)

A very simple but extremely versatile sauce: great on its own over some pasta with Parmesan, easily enhanced by adding a few more ingredients, or used as the start of other dishes.

> Serves 4
> *1 medium-sized onion*
> *4 cloves of garlic, minced*
> *1 stick of celery, chopped finely*
> *1 medium carrot, chopped finely*
> *1 x 400 g chopped tomatoes*
> *1 tbsp tomato puree*
> *200 ml water (use it to rinse the tins)*
> *Olive oil*
> *½ tsp rosemary*
> *½ tsp thyme*
> *1 bay leaf*

Chop the onion finely and fry together with the minced garlic in olive oil until transparent. Put in the carrots and celery and sweat for another 8 minutes before adding chopped tomatoes, tomato puree, herbs and a good pinch of sugar. Cover with a lid, bring to the boil, then turn heat down and leave to simmer for at least 1 hour, stirring from time to time.

Once the sauce has cooked, add ½ to 1 level tsp salt and ½ tsp of freshly grated pepper. Discard the bay leaf.

Leave chunky or blend to a smooth sauce.

Pasta sauce variation:
The sauce can be easily enhanced by adding:
 – some pan-fried mushrooms and freshly chopped chilli
 – a drained tin of sardines, some olives and capers
 – some pan-fried pieces of pork sausage
 – some diced feta, olives, freshly chopped basil and a good drizzle of olive oil
   to top the pasta and sauce

We also use this sauce in our ratatouille recipe (page 84)

Mushroom barley-sotto (Wheat free, optionally VEGAN)

An adaptation of the traditional risotto. The chewy barley gives it a good bite and makes for a wholesome meal together with a big green salad.

Serves 4
1 medium onion, finely chopped
Olive oil
2 sticks of celery, washed and finely chopped
1 medium carrot, scraped, finely chopped
2 cloves of garlic, finely minced
270 g of pearl barley
1 glass of dry white wine (we do not use wine at the Abbey but I do at home –
*   it enhances the flavour of the dish. If cooking without wine, add 1 tsp of white*
*   wine vinegar or lemon juice at the end of the cooking process)*
600 g mushrooms – use the traditional white button mushrooms or, for a
*   deeper flavour, wild mushrooms or shiitake – roughly chopped. At home I have*
*   successfully cooked with rehydrated wild mushrooms – use about 60 g of dried*
*   produce and soak them for at least 30 min before cooking.*
3 large tomatoes – skinned* and chopped or 1 tbsp tomato puree
1 tsp dried rosemary or a 10 cm sprig fresh rosemary
1 large bay leaf
300-400 ml vegetable stock (depending on how much the barley absorbs)
1 heaped tbsp butter
2 tbsp grated Parmesan cheese
Salt and pepper

For vegan/dairy free diets: Omit butter and cheese. Serve instead topped with extra virgin olive oil and some toasted walnuts.

* To skin a tomato: Place into a heatproof bowl. Pour boiling water over it and leave for 30 seconds. Drain, then score the skin with a pointy knife and start peeling it off.

Clean the mushrooms with a knife and some kitchen paper. (Do not wash them as they will absorb lots of water which will dilute their taste.) Heat up a solid-based pan with sunflower oil until hot – add mushrooms and fry on a high heat until browned, adding some more oil if necessary. When done, scoop out, wipe the pan carefully with kitchen paper, then fry the onions on a low to medium heat in olive oil until transparent but not browned. Add garlic, carrots and celery and continue cooking for another 2 minutes, stirring regularly. Add the barley and stir-fry for 1 minute before adding the wine if using. Leave to cook until most of the liquid is gone, then add a ladleful of the vegetable stock, tomatoes (or puree), bay leaf and rosemary. (If omitting the wine, just continue straight with adding stock and other ingredients.)

Bring to the boil – you can do this on high heat but make sure to stay with it and stir all the time to avoid burning. When boiling, turn heat down until the food is just simmering. Stir from time to time – I tend to set a 5-minute timer if I am busy elsewhere … Once it starts thickening, add more stock and keep on cooking on low heat, adding even more liquid if necessary, until the barley has swollen and is soft with a bite and the dish has a porridgy, slightly runny consistency. Add the mushrooms before taking the pan off the heat.

Stir through the butter. Once it is melted, add the grated Parmesan (the melted butter – or other dairy-like cream added – will ensure that the cheese dissolves into the dish rather than stays stringy). If you want to keep it dairy free, just stir through some dairy free cream or cream cheese alternative.

Remove the bay leaf, and add a good amount of freshly grated pepper and salt to taste.

This dish can be adapted to your heart's content. Replace mushrooms, tomatoes and rosemary with:

- a medium-sized (butternut) squash, peeled, diced and roasted (200 C (400 F) static/180 C (350 F) fan/gas 6) with olive oil and salt until soft. Add this, together with 1 tsp sage, halfway through cooking time.
- 2 fist-sized beetroot – roasted in the oven (200 C (400 F) static/180 C (350 F) fan/gas 6), skin on, until tender. Peel, dice, add to the mix together with the first batch of stock. Instead of Parmesan, use blue cheese, such as Stilton.
- leftover ratatouille, added towards the end of the cooking time.
- a mix of fresh green garden vegetables like spinach, leeks, broccoli – separately stir-fried until just cooked and only added at the end for the last 2 minutes to avoid overcooking.

It is also good left plain, served with a big mixed salad or/and bean fritters, fried fish or meat.

Garlic roast courgette lasagne

A brilliant dish to make in advance, or even freeze, before baking. This is quite a light lasagne, using lots of courgettes which reduces the amount of white sauce needed.

> Serves 4
> *1 kg courgettes, preferably small and firm, as they have more flavour*
> *½ bulb of garlic, finely chopped*
> *Olive oil*
> *80 g plain white flour*
> *80 g butter*
> *800 ml full fat milk*
> *1 bay leaf*
> *½ tsp freshly grated nutmeg*
> *Salt*
> *250 g lasagne sheets*
> *100 g mature Cheddar cheese*

Start by roasting the courgettes: Preheat your oven to 220 C (425 F) static/200 C (400 F) fan/gas 7. Wash the courgettes, cut into slices just under 1 cm thick, and place into a big metal roasting dish. Mix the finely chopped garlic with 100 ml olive oil, pour over the courgettes, then toss so that all the slices are covered in the oil. Place into the hot oven and roast for 20-25 minutes until the courgettes start to brown and soften.

Leave the oven on if you want to cook the lasagne today, but turn it down to 190 C (375 F) static/170 C (340 F) fan/gas 5.

During the roasting process you can start making the bechamel sauce: In a heavy-based pan melt the butter on a low to medium heat – you don't want to brown it. Add the bay leaf and leave to simmer on a low heat for 2 minutes for the bay leaf to infuse. Turn up the heat to medium, add the flour and stir into a paste (also called roux), cooking it for a minute while stirring constantly. Have the milk ready to add (or take the pan off the heat while you are preparing it). Increase the heat slightly. Pour ⅓ of the milk into the pan, stirring constantly and mixing the roux with the milk which will slowly start to thicken. Don't worry too much if there are lumps at this stage – you will be able to stir them away during the cooking process.

Add more milk once the sauce starts getting thick until all is used up. Bring to the boil while stirring constantly. Turn down the heat if you feel the sauce starting to catch on the bottom. (If heavily stuck, it's better to pour it into another pan to continue as it will be hard to avoid burning the sauce, which affects the flavour.) Once boiling, turn down to a simmer, leave for just 1 minute, then take off the heat. Season the sauce with nutmeg and 1 tsp salt or more to taste – it needs to be quite robust as both courgettes and pasta are unsalted.

To assemble the lasagne grease a suitable ceramic or metal baking dish, about 20 x 30 cm in size.

Pour some bechamel sauce into the bottom, just enough to cover the base thinly, then put down the first layer of lasagne sheets, followed by a few spoonfuls of bechamel sauce, spread out to a thin layer, and courgettes. Place the latter slice by slice with no space inbetween. Add the next layer of lasagne sheets, then continue with some sauce, courgettes, etc, until all courgettes are used up – you should get about 3 courgette layers out of it. Finish with one last layer of pasta and pour the rest of the bechamel sauce on top, spreading it so that all the sheets are covered. If there is any liquid left in the courgette roasting tray, scrape this over the lasagne, too – there is a lot of flavour in it.

At this stage you could let it cool down and leave it covered in the fridge for up to three days, or freeze it.

If using today, place into the preheated oven at 180 C (350 F) static/160 C (320 F) fan/gas 4-5 and bake for 30 minutes. Then take it out and sprinkle with grated Cheddar (though any strong-flavoured cheese will do – it will taste amazing with a mix of Stilton and Cheddar) and put back into the oven to bake for a further 10 minutes.

If using the lasagne the next day from cold, bake for 50 minutes, adding the cheese after 40 minutes.

Squash and walnut lasagne: This recipe also works really well with roast squash (butternut or any of those other beautiful cucurbits that are for sale these days in the late summer and autumn months). Use about 900 g peeled weight, the squash cut into small, about 1 cm, dice. Toss in olive oil and lots of garlic and roast for 15-25 minutes at 220 C (425 F) static/200 C (400 F) fan/gas 7 until soft and slightly browned at the edges.

In the same oven, toast two handfuls of walnut halves for 5-7 minutes. Chop these roughly.

Layer the lasagne in the same way as in the recipe above, sprinkling some of the nuts over each squash layer.

Pasta bake with cashews, mushrooms, greens and a bread crust (VEGAN, optionally GF)

A creamy cashew sauce replaces the more traditional bechamel sauce for a delicious vegan pasta bake. The vegetables can easily be varied – pre-cooked mushrooms, broccoli, courgettes, aubergines will all work well.

Serves 2-3

200 g wholewheat penne or spirals, or GF pasta such as brown rice pasta

Sauce:
100 g cashew nuts
1 tbsp olive oil
1 bay leaf
1 large white onion, chopped finely
1 clove of garlic, minced
½ tsp turmeric
300 ml water
1 level tsp salt
1 level tsp Dijon mustard
1 tsp lemon juice, to taste
½ tsp freshly grated nutmeg
1 red pepper, washed and diced
100 g spinach, kale or Swiss chard, washed and roughly chopped if necessary
2 thick slices of bread (wheat or gluten free)

Soak the cashews for a minimum of 4 hours, or overnight, in plenty of water.

Preheat the oven to 200 C (400 F) static/180 C (350 F) fan/gas 6.

In a heavy-based small pan heat the olive oil, then add onion, garlic and bay leaf, cooking these over a medium heat until transparent – this will take 10 minutes. Discard the bay leaf.

Add the drained nuts, turmeric, 300 ml of hot water and 1 level tsp of salt. Bring to boil, then cook for 2 minutes. Using a soup blender or kitchen processor, blend the nuts and liquid to a smooth sauce. This will take quite a while – I had best results with a jug blender. Add lemon juice, nutmeg and mustard to the sauce, some freshly ground pepper, and more salt if needed. Put aside.

In a new pan, on medium heat, stir-fry the diced pepper in olive oil for 5 minutes, then add the chosen greens and cook until just wilted. Scrape into the sauce and mix well.

Cook the pasta per packet cooking instructions in well-salted water until just al dente (with bite). Drain, then mix with the prepared sauce and turn into an ovenproof dish.

Using your kitchen processor, whizz the bread, torn into smaller pieces first, into breadcrumbs. Sprinkle on top of the pasta, then bake in the preheated oven for 20-30 minutes.

Moroccan vegetable tagine (GF, VEGAN)

Inspired by the excellent food I ate during a holiday to Morocco, this recipe doesn't only taste wonderful, it looks great with its colourful selection of vegetables in a rich red sauce. Try to find preserved lemons in a larger supermarket or a Middle Eastern grocer – they really add to the flavour.

> Serves 4
> *1 small or ½ large butternut squash, peeled and cut into 1.5 cm dice*
> *1 large aubergine, washed and cut into 2 cm dice*
> *2 courgettes (about 20 cm long), washed and thickly sliced*
> *100 g dried chickpeas, soaked overnight in plenty of water with a good pinch of*
>   *bicarbonate of soda, or 1 x 400 g tin (240 g drained weight) of cooked chickpeas*
> *1 large onion, finely chopped*
> *2 cm chunky piece of fresh ginger, grated, or 1 tsp dried ginger*
> *3 cloves of garlic, finely chopped*
> *1½ tsp ground coriander*
> *2 tsp ground cumin*
> *1 tsp caraway seeds*
> *½ tsp turmeric*
> *Good pinch of chilli flakes or chilli powder (increase or decrease depending on your*
>   *taste)*
> *1 x 400 g tin chopped tomatoes*
> *6 whole dried apricots, chopped into quarters*
> *½ tsp honey*
> *500 ml vegetable stock*
> *1 level tsp salt, ½ tsp freshly ground pepper*
> *2 small preserved lemons or 1 tbsp lemon juice*
> *Fresh coriander to serve*

Preheat your oven to 200 C (400 F) static/180 C (350 F) fan/gas 6.

If using dried chickpeas, drain them after having soaked overnight in plenty of water. Place into a suitable pan, cover with fresh cold water, bring to boil and cook for 20-40 minutes, or even longer (depending on the freshness of the chickpeas) until soft – you want to be able to squish them easily between your fingers. Don't rush this process.

If using tinned chickpeas, drain, wash and put aside.

Place all of your dried spices into a cast iron casserole (any vessel that can be used on the hob and in the oven will do), and toast on a medium heat until they smell fragrant – stay with it or they might burn and taste bitter. Scrape into a bowl and put aside.

Heat a little sunflower oil in the same saucepan and sweat the onions and garlic until they become translucent. Add the spice powder, grated ginger, chopped tomatoes, honey, apricots and vegetable stock. Cover pan with a lid, bring to the boil and then simmer on a low heat for 1 hour, stirring from time to time.

Meanwhile, place butternut squash and aubergines into a large, deep roasting tin, toss them in 3-4 tbsp sunflower oil until coated and place into the preheated oven together with an ovenproof vessel filled with hot water. The water will prevent the aubergines drying out during the roasting process – especially important in fan ovens.

Roast for 20 minutes, then add the courgettes, toss them in the oil which should have gathered in the bottom of the pan (if not, add a bit more oil), then roast for a further 20-30 minutes until the courgettes are browned.

When the tomato sauce has cooked, add the cooked chickpeas, roast vegetables and the finely chopped peel of one of the preserved lemons (discard the soft inside). If you do not have preserved lemons at hand, use 1 tbsp lemon juice instead. Stir and bring back to boil on a medium heat.

Serve sprinkled with fresh coriander and the finely chopped peel of the second preserved lemon. Traditionally, a tagine would be eaten with flatbread, big chunks torn off the loaf and dipped into the food. It is just as good with couscous (or quinoa for gluten free diets) or brown rice.

Butter bean fritters with chard and cranberries
(optionally GF and DF)

Best eaten fresh, these are substantial and full of flavour. They make a great summer lunch with a big leafy salad on the side, or a satisfying winter meal served with roast root vegetables such as baby potatoes, celeriac, beetroot, carrots and parsnips.

Serves 4

2 eggs, beaten
50 ml milk (or dairy free alternative)
50 g self-raising flour (or gluten free self-raising flour)
25 g cornflour
50 g Parmesan or Stilton (omit for dairy free diets)
1 tbsp dried cranberries (or barberries, available from Middle Eastern grocers)
2 tsp Dijon mustard
100 g chard or spinach (frozen will work, too)
4 spring onions, finely chopped
180 g dried butter beans, soaked overnight in plenty of water with a big pinch of
   bicarbonate of soda, or 2 x 400 g tins of butter beans (drained and washed)
70 ml extra milk or DF alternative for mashing beans
Sunflower oil for frying

Wash and drain the beans well. Put into a pan with fresh cold water and boil until extremely soft, almost falling apart – that will take up to an hour.

Drain, put back into the pan, add the 70 ml extra liquid and using a potato masher turn into a lumpy mush.

Chop the chard, stir-fry quickly until just wilted. Discard any liquid.

In a large bowl beat together eggs, milk, flour and cornflour to a smooth batter. Stir in the spring onions, beans, cheese, mustard, cranberries and stir-fried chard.

Heat up a frying pan for 1 minute on medium heat, add 1 tbsp sunflower oil, and without over-crowding the pan, add a heaped tablespoon-worth of mixture and fry for 2-3 minutes on each side (don't rush the process).

Serve fritters straight away with tomato and chilli sauce (page 94), a fresh tomato salsa (page 68) or sweet chilli sauce.

Ratatouille with rosemary and Parmesan roast polenta (GF, optionally VEGAN)

Two great Mediterranean staples which go well together, but can also be made on their own and served with different sides: the polenta goes well with any other stew, or even just a big mixed salad for a light lunch. The ratatouille is just as good served with bread, rice, potatoes or pasta.

Serves 4
For the polenta:
170 g medium polenta
875 ml of water
1 tsp dried rosemary or 1 dessertspoon freshly chopped rosemary
1 heaped tsp salt
30 g butter (for a dairy free option, replace with olive oil)
40 g grated parmesan or any other hard cheese (omit for dairy free polenta)

Sprinkle a 25 x 25 cm roasting dish/ceramic dish with water – this will prevent the polenta from sticking.

Traditionally one makes polenta by bringing water to the boil and then slowly adding the grain, while whisking all the time to avoid lumps. While I try to whisk very fast, I have not yet managed to produce a satisfactorily smooth mix! Therefore I put the polenta, water, rosemary and salt into a heavy-based saucepan, heating it up first on medium to high heat, then, once it starts getting hot, on medium heat, stirring all the time, until thickened and continuously bubbling. Simmer for a further 5 minutes, stirring constantly.

Be careful not to get burned by erupting polenta – wear a long-sleeved top and oven gloves.

Take off the heat, stir in the butter, then the Parmesan (the butter helps the cheese melt into the polenta rather than staying a stringy mass). Without delay (the mix starts setting quite quickly) pour into the water-sprinkled dish and smooth out the surface. Put aside for at least one hour to set.

Meanwhile, prepare the ratatouille:

1 portion basic tomato sauce (see page 73)
1 level tsp ground coriander
Salt and pepper
2 large aubergines
3 red or yellow peppers
4 firm small courgettes, about 15 cm long
Olive oil

Preheat the oven to 200 C (400 F) static/180 C (350 F) fan/gas 6.

Place an ovenproof dish filled with water into the preheating oven – this will prevent the aubergines from drying out during the roasting process.

Prepare the tomato sauce (see page 73) adding 1 level tsp of ground coriander to the mix.

While the tomato sauce is cooking, wash the remaining vegetables, cut courgettes into thick slices, peppers into chunky pieces and aubergines into 1 inch cubes. Put the diced aubergine into a large baking tray, add 2 tbsp olive oil, sprinkle with salt, then roast in the preheated oven (BE CAREFUL – hot steam will escape on first opening) for 15 minutes. Meanwhile, in a bowl, toss peppers and courgettes in 1-2 tbsp olive oil.

Carefully take the tray with aubergines out of the oven, then add peppers and courgettes, and roast for a further 20 minutes – by then the aubergines should be soft and squishy, the peppers and courgettes soft and browned at the edges. Once the tomato sauce has been made, leave it chunky, add the roasted vegetables, 1 level tsp salt and 1 tsp pepper and stir through. Taste and adjust.

Pour the ratatouille into a suitable roasting dish (one of the ones you prepared your vegetables in might do and save you the washing up), then cover with aluminium foil and put aside.

Back to the polenta: Preheat the oven to 200 C (400 F) static/180 C (350 F) fan/gas 6 if not still hot from roasting the vegetables.

Cover the dish containing the polenta with a chopping board and turn over – the block should release onto the board. Cut into 9 pieces. Brush a baking tray with olive oil, place the pieces of polenta on top, leaving at least 1 cm space between each. Brush each piece with olive oil, then place into the still hot oven at temperature above for 35-40 minutes to roast until browned and crisp.

Assuming the ratatouille is still warm at this point, place the dish into the same oven for the last 20 minutes of roasting. If cold, it will need at least 30 minutes of reheating.

Home-made baked beans (GF, VEGAN)

A British staple, richer in taste and less sweet than its tinned cousins. Give it a try, even if you love your favourite tinned version.

Traditionally made with cannellini beans, but really almost any bean will do … for the picture we used pinto beans.

Serves 6-8
*360 g of dried beans, soaked overnight in plenty of water together with a pinch of
    bicarbonate of soda*
or 2 x 400 g tins of your favourite beans

If using dried beans: Drain, place into a pan and cover with fresh cold water. Bring to a boil and keep on cooking until the beans are very soft – you want to be able to squish them easily between your fingers. This process will take up to an hour, depending on the freshness of the beans. Once cooked, drain, then set aside until needed.

Tomato sauce:
1 red onion
2 cloves of garlic
Olive oil
100 g tomato puree
½ tsp vegetable stock powder or ⅓ of a vegetable stock cube
300 ml apple juice
150 ml water
2 tsp black treacle or molasses
1 level tsp salt
½ tsp grated nutmeg
¼ tsp ground cloves (or 3 whole cloves)
½ tsp cinnamon
½ tsp dried dill
1 bay leaf
1 tsp tamari sauce or soy sauce
½ tsp freshly milled pepper

Fry finely chopped onions and garlic in olive oil until soft, then add all the other sauce ingredients (bar the pepper and beans). Cover with a lid, bring to boil, then simmer for 1½ hours on a low heat. Stir from time to time. If too thick in consistency, add some more water. Remove bay leaf and blend to a smooth sauce with a soup blender, or using a kitchen processor.

Mix with the cooked beans and pepper, stir through, taste and add more salt if necessary.

These beans are excellent with a baked potato or on a thick slab of buttered wholemeal toast.

Vegetable crumble with seeds

Cranks 'oh so delicious' leek croustade has been a long-time favourite at the Abbey. The nutty, cheesy base covered by a creamy leek and tomato topping always converts the most avid meat eaters. The following dish is an adaptation, using seeds instead of nuts, substituting vegetables, and turning both layers upside down.

Serves 4-5
Crumble:
200 g fresh wholemeal breadcrumbs
60 g soft butter
120 g mature Cheddar cheese, grated
50 g pumpkin seeds
50 g sunflower seeds
25 g sesame seeds
½ tsp thyme
½ tsp salt

Place all the above into a mixing bowl and, using your hands, rub the fat into the breadcrumbs and seeds. Put aside.

Vegetable base:
2 medium-sized sweet potatoes, about 300 g each in weight
4 golf-ball-sized new potatoes
1 small head of broccoli
Olive or sunflower oil for roasting
½ tsp salt

Preheat an oven to 220 (425 F) static/200 C (400 F) fan/gas 7.

Scrub the sweet potatoes, wash the new potatoes, leaving on the skin of both, cut into 1½ cm cubes, toss lightly in oil and place into a 20 x 30 cm or 25 cm diameter deep ovenproof dish: the one you want to serve it in.

Sprinkle with ½ tsp salt, then roast at one of the above temperatures until browned at the edges and soft – this will take 25-30 minutes. If you are pre-preparing the dish for later, turn the oven off now, otherwise leave it on to bake the dish.

Cut the top of the broccoli into small florets, and slice the thick stalk after peeling off the tough outer layer.

Place into a small pan together with 200 ml water. Cover with a well-fitting lid, bring to boil and steam for 4 minutes. Drain and scatter over the potatoes once they have come out of the oven.

Sauce:
1 medium-sized leek
70 g butter or 70 ml olive oil
50 g wholemeal flour
500 ml milk
1 bay leaf
Salt, pepper, lemon juice, grated nutmeg

After washing the leek well (I usually slash it open lengthways and soak it for a bit before cleaning it under running cold water), chop up into slices, using ALL the green parts that are not withered (the green gives colour and taste).

In a heavy-based pan, melt the butter, then add bay leaf and leeks and fry on a low to medium heat until wilted but not browned. Add flour and stir in, then pour in the milk, stirring all the time. When the sauce starts thickening, turn down heat slightly, and keep on stirring until the sauce starts bubbling – let it boil for a further minute while stirring constantly. Take off the heat, remove the bay leaf, and season with ½ tsp salt, ½ tsp freshly ground pepper, ½ tsp nutmeg and 1 tsp lemon juice. Taste and adjust if necessary.

Pour over the potatoes, sweet potatoes and broccoli and carefully stir through it with a spatula to coat all the vegetables with the sauce.

Scatter the crumble mixture over the top.

You can stop here and bake the crumble later (35-40 minutes in a preheated oven at 200 C (400 F) static/180 C (350 F) fan/gas 6) or bake it now at the same temperature for 25-30 minutes until golden brown.

Serve with a leafy salad.

Vegetable and peanut stew (GF, VEGAN)

A rich and warming casserole, with its ingredients inspired by West African cooking. This recipe uses okra, a vegetable of good flavour but also interesting texture. It's important not to overcook it, or it becomes rather slimy – use green beans if okra is not available or not to your liking.

Serves 4
1 medium onion
3 cloves of garlic
A good pinch of chilli flakes or chilli powder, more if you like your food hot
3 cm piece of fresh ginger root (or 1 tsp ground ginger)
2 tsp curry powder such as Madras
1 tin of chopped tomatoes
400 ml water
1 tsp vegetable stock powder or one stock cube
½ cup of unsweetened peanut butter (go for one without palm oil)
1 large sweet potato – about 600 g in weight, or similar weight of peeled butternut squash
2 large carrots
300 g fresh or frozen okra – if available; if not, replace with French green beans or runner beans
½ small turnip/swede/rutabaga
250 g of spinach, fresh or frozen
Vegetable oil for roasting and frying
Salt, pepper
Lemon juice

Chop the onions and garlic finely. Scrub the carrots and cut into thick slices. Peel the sweet potato and swede and cut into 2 cm dice. Wash the spinach and drain.

Wash the okra and cut each into 3 pieces. (If using green beans, cut into bite-size pieces, bring a pan of water to the boil, add beans, bring back to boil and cook for 4 minutes. Drain and put aside.)

Preheat the oven to 200 C (400 F) static/180 C (350 F) fan/gas 6.

Heat 2 tbsp sunflower oil in a heavy-based larger pan, then add the onions, frying them until transparent and lightly browned. Add ginger, garlic and spices, stir-fry for a further minute, then add tomatoes, water, vegetable stock powder. Cover the pan with a lid and bring to boil. Once boiling, turn down the heat to a simmer and leave to cook covered for at least 1 hour. Stir from time to time.

Meanwhile, place the carrots, turnips and sweet potatoes in an ovenproof dish, toss them in 1-2 tbsp vegetable oil and roast in the preheated oven for 30-40 minutes or until the vegetables are soft.

When the sauce has cooked, take off the heat, add the peanut butter, then blend it all to a smooth consistency with a stick blender or in a kitchen machine.

Put back onto a medium heat, add spinach and okra, bring gently back to the boil and cook for a further 5 minutes, stirring all the time to avoid burning.

(If using green beans, add those in the next step with the roast vegetables.)

Add the roast vegetables, 1 dessertspoon of lemon juice and ½ tsp salt.

Stir, taste and adjust seasoning if necessary. If the dish seems to have cooled a bit by now, heat through again, then serve. It's lovely served on a bed of brown rice.

Nut, buckwheat and mushroom roast with a tomato and chilli sauce (VEGAN, optionally GF)

A veggie staple for special meals, this delivers a hearty, crunchy dish – 'something to chew on' – a quality a lot of meat-eaters miss in vegetarian food.

Buckwheat is still a little-used ingredient here in Britain. It is a pseudo grain (nothing to do with wheat, so it is free of gluten) related to sorrel, knotweed and rhubarb. Widely used in Russia and the whole of Asia, it has a robust flavour, offers protein and is very nutritious. If it's not your thing or you can't get hold of it, use the same amount of nuts instead.

Serves 4
1 medium onion or 1 small leek, finely chopped
1 clove of garlic, minced
1 tbsp butter or olive oil
100 g button mushrooms, wiped and finely chopped
150 g chopped mixed nuts, or whole mixed nuts chopped roughly in a food processor
100 g buckwheat groats
80 g gluten free or wheat bread – whizzed to crumbs in a kitchen machine
220 ml vegetable stock
1 tsp thyme
½-1 level tsp salt
½ tsp cracked pepper

Preheat the oven to 190 C (375 F) static/170 C (340 F) fan/gas 5.

Place the chopped nuts and buckwheat groats into a baking tray. Place this into the preheating oven and toast for about 15-25 minutes – depending on how quickly your oven heats up – until lightly browned. Set yourself a timer and check regularly to avoid burning, which will happen quite suddenly due to the high oil content in the nuts.

Heat up a medium saucepan for a minute – you want to make sure it is hot so the onion or leek, garlic and mushrooms, once added, will start frying immediately. Add a splash of sunflower oil and stir-fry for 1-2 min on a high heat until lightly browned.

Add the vegetable stock, salt, pepper, thyme and breadcrumbs, and bring to a boil, stirring all of the time. Cook for 30 seconds on a medium heat, continuing to stir.

Now add your nuts and buckwheat groats – a sticky mixture will form. Take it off the heat. Taste, and add more salt if necessary.

Grease a 900 g/2 lb loaf tin with oil and line the bottom with baking parchment. Press the mixture into this and flatten on top.

Place into the preheated oven and bake for 25-35 min until golden brown on top.

After baking, let it stand for a few minutes, then turn it out of the tin (you might have to loosen the edges by going round them with a dinner knife), cut into thick pieces and serve on a bed of tomato and chilli sauce (next recipe).

This mixture also makes a very good stuffing for peppers, or courgettes that have grown into marrows. Just deseed the vegetables, fill with the nutty mix and roast for 30-40 min. Serve with the tomato and chilli sauce.

Tomato and chilli sauce

This is an easy to make, versatile sauce, great with the above nut roast, with the bean fritters (page 82), or as a quick pasta sauce. It's worth making double the amount and freezing the rest for another occasion. You can always omit the chilli if you prefer a milder sauce. It's great with cranberries added at the end.

Serves 4-6
1 small onion, chopped
4 cloves of garlic, minced
1 x 400 g tin chopped tomatoes
250 ml vegetable stock
1 bay leaf
1 level tsp soft brown sugar
½ tsp pepper
½ tsp salt
As much chopped fresh chilli as you like, or chilli flakes
Optional: 1 tbsp cranberries, finely chopped

Fry onions and garlic in some olive oil until transparent but not browned. Add thyme, a bay leaf, the chopped tomatoes and sugar. Cover the pot with a lid and bring the sauce to the boil.

Once boiling, cook for at least 45 minutes on low heat – this will sweeten the taste and let the flavours mingle. Check from time to time, stirring and adding more water if it seems to become too thick. You can chop the chilli finely during this time.

After cooking, take the sauce off the heat, fish out the bay leaf (important) and blend to a smooth consistency with a stick blender or in a kitchen processor.

Put the sauce back on the heat, add your preferred amount of chilli. (I like little pockets of heat in something milder – better than a hot sauce. If you prefer the latter, add the chilli earlier in the cooking process.) Also add salt and pepper (and the cranberries if wanted) and bring back to a boil for 1 minute. Taste and adjust, then serve.

Falafel (GF, VEGAN)

Like the hummus, this recipe came to the Abbey kitchen through Hanna, a Palestinian volunteer. He would make them often, not necessarily to feed the guests, but just as a snack for all the staff. He loved preparing those crunchy morsels – and we loved eating them. Sometimes I would see him chatting with some Abbey visitors out on the grounds, a wee bowl of falafel with him to offer around.

My colleague Shuggie, who had a staunch dislike of chickpeas, didn't need much convincing to eat them!

You will need a good kitchen processor to make these.

> Makes 16-18 falafel – feeds 4 for main course, 6 for snacks
> *250 g dried chickpeas (do not use tinned ones!)*
> *1 medium onion*
> *1 clove of garlic*
> *A handful of parsley, stalks and leaves, chopped*
> *1 level tsp ground cumin*
> *1 tsp sea salt*
> *1 level tbsp gram (chickpea) flour – or if not at hand, plain flour will do*
> *Sunflower oil (or groundnut oil) for deep-frying*

Soak the chickpeas for at least 8 hours – so best overnight – in about 1 litre of cold water together with 1 level tsp of bicarbonate of soda (the soda makes the water more alkaline and helps soften the chickpeas).

The next day drain and rinse, discard any discoloured specimens, then place the good chickpeas into the bowl of the kitchen processor with the blending blade attached. Chop onions, garlic and parsley finely and add to the chickpeas, together with cumin and salt.

Blend on high speed to a coarse mush, stopping the machine halfway through to scrape down any big bits from the sides. Scrape the mix into a bowl and leave for at least 1 hour to rest in the fridge or a cool place – this allows the starch in the mix to swell and bind it all together.

We have had good results baking our falafel in the oven (see below); however, to achieve the best falafel, deep-fry them:

Use a deep-fryer, or fill a medium-sized tall saucepan with sunflower oil to 6 cm deep – do not overfill it, or it might spill over once it gets hot and you add the falafel mix. Take special care if you are using a gas cooker, as the open flame and hot oil present a huge fire risk – have a fire blanket ready!

Heat the oil to 180 C (356 F) – an electronic or jam thermometer comes in handy here. Also, pre-heat your oven to around 100 C (212 F) – you want it ready to keep the cooked falafel warm while you fry the rest.

Once hot, take heaped teaspoonsful of falafel mix and press each one in your hand with the tea-spoon into an egg shape. The mixture won't seem very cohesive, and shaping it might be a bit fiddly, but persist – it will work!

Lower the pieces carefully on the spoon into the hot fat.

Do not overfill the pan – this will cool down the oil too much which will make the end product greasy – 4-5 pieces is optimal. Cook for 3-4 minutes until well browned and cooked through. Fish out the pieces with a slotted spoon, and drain on a kitchen-paper-lined cooling rack or colander; then place in a dish in the preheated oven to keep warm while you finish frying the rest of the mix.

They are best served fresh and go nicely with Tzatziki (page 56) or dipped into tahini dressing (page 70), together with a big salad.

Oven-baked falafel: Preheat oven to 220 C (425 F) static/200 C (400 F) fan/gas 7. Make the falafel mix as described above. Take a large piece of baking parchment, scrunch it up, then unfold and line a deep 20 x 30 cm baking tray, with paper overhanging the sides of the tray – this will make cleaning up easier.

Pour deep-frying oil into the tray to a depth of 1 cm. Place the tray in the preheated oven for 7 minutes to heat up (use a timer – you don't want to overheat the oil). Meanwhile, start shaping falafel, by moulding the mix into 16-18 little patties. The mix will feel fragile, just press hard together and place gently on a board.

Now take the tray with oil CAREFULLY out of the oven. Place on a stable surface, place falafel into the hot oil, using a cake slice or similar, and move the tray back into the oven. Set a timer for 15 minutes.

After 15 minutes, take the tray out of the oven and, using a cake slice or fork, turn the falafel over. Place back into the oven for another 15 minutes.

Kale and lemon pesto (GF, optionally VEGAN/DF)

Extremely hardy and fast growing, kale plants supply many island folk with tasty and healthy greens throughout three quarters of the year. Besides being a nourishing side vegetable, it also makes great pesto.

Serves 4-6
100 g kale, preferably smaller leaves, thick fibrous stems cut out
Zest of 1 unwaxed lemon
Juice of ½ lemon
1 small clove of garlic
½ tsp salt
*60 g whole almonds (you can take the skin off by soaking them for an hour in
    warm water)*
50 ml olive oil
30 ml cold water
30 g Parmesan (omit if you want to keep it dairy free/vegan)

Bring a small pan of water and 1 tsp of salt to the boil, add the kale and blanch for 30 seconds, then drain and cool down immediately with running cold water from the tap to stop it cooking more. Drain well.

Place into a jug-style kitchen processor, together with the zest of lemon, lemon juice, garlic, salt, almonds, olive oil and water. Blend to a smooth consistency. Scrape the pesto into a bowl, add finely grated parmesan if wanted, then taste and add more salt if needed.

To serve, toss with freshly cooked pasta and other vegetables, such as cooked broccoli and peas, or use it as a luxurious topping for pizza or a risotto.

The pesto will keep, stored in an airtight container in the fridge, for up to a week, or for up to 3 months in the freezer.

Egg fried rice (GF, DF)

Another simple but utterly delicious dish – Shakila, a young volunteer from Sri Lanka, taught me the recipe. It's good on its own with a crunchy salad – the Waldorf (page 62) goes really well with it. However, if you are into 'fusion food', try it with grilled black pudding: our local Mull black pudding, or the ones from Stornoway or Bury (thanks, Jim, for introducing us to it!) are excellent.

> *Serves 4 on its own, or 5-6 if accompanied with a big salad and/or black pudding*
> *300 g brown or white long grain rice such as basmati*
> *1 bay leaf*
> *2 whole cloves*
> *1 large leek*
> *2 medium carrots*
> *2 cloves of garlic*
> *½ tsp turmeric*
> *⅓ tsp ground cloves*
> *2-3 tsp Madras curry powder*
> *1 level tsp salt*
> *Toasted sesame oil*
> *3 eggs*
> *Wedges of lemon or lime to serve*

Traditionally egg fried rice is made with leftover rice from the day before, so if making it on the day, make sure to prepare it well in advance so it has time to cool fully.

Cook the rice according to the packet instructions together with a bay leaf and 2 whole cloves. Leave to cool fully, covered with a tea towel.

Next, prepare the vegetables: Wash the leek thoroughly, trim off any withered bits but do not cut off the firm dark green leaves. Halve lengthwise and then slice very thinly. Scrub or peel the carrots, and grate roughly into julienne strips – best with a mandoline grater (though the biggest holes in a box grater will do, too).

Break the eggs into a bowl and whisk with a fork.

Heat a large, heavy-based (cast iron works well) frying pan or wok for 2 minutes, then add 2 tbsp toasted sesame oil, the leeks and the carrots, stir-frying for 1-2 minutes until the leeks have just wilted but still have their vivid green colour. Turn down to a low heat.

In its pan, stir up the rice to squash any lumps, discard the bay leaf and cloves, then add to the frying pan, heating the rice through while stirring all the time. If the rice seems to get stuck on the base, turn down the heat even more.

Once the rice seems hot, add all the spices and salt, and stir through until well distributed.

Scrape the rice mix to the sides of the pan or wok, to expose part of the base about the size of the palm of your hand. Add a little sesame oil. Pour in the egg and leave to set for 1 minute or so, then start stirring, scrambling it lightly without yet incorporating too much rice – this will take a wee while. Once the egg is cooked to a dry scramble, break it up into small pieces with your wooden spoon and stir through the rice. Serve immediately with the wedges of lemon or lime on the side.

Vegetables and dahl (GF, VEGAN)

This could be a very simple and quick midweek meal, served with rice or naan, or by choosing a wide range of vegetables and adding some other bits and bobs, it could become a vegetarian feast to share with your friends over a long, sociable evening.

> Serves 4
> *First make the dahl:*
> *1 medium onion, finely chopped*
> *2 cloves of garlic, minced*
> *½ tsp of turmeric*
> *1 level tsp cumin seeds (or ground cumin)*
> *1 bay leaf*
> *300 g red lentils*
> *1 litre vegetable stock or water*
> *Salt, pepper, lemon juice*

Heat up a medium pan until hot, then add the cumin seeds and roast until fragrant – do not burn them or they will taste bitter. Add 1 tbsp vegetable oil and the onions and fry until transparent. Add garlic, turmeric, bay leaf, lentils and the vegetable stock or hot water from the kettle. Cover with a lid and bring to a boil. Once boiling, turn down to lowest heat, and cook for 20-30 minutes until thickened and the lentils are falling apart. Stir from time to time to make sure the lentils do not stick to the base of the pan. Add more water if necessary. When finished cooking, add 1 tsp of lemon juice and 1-1½ tsp salt (more salt if you use water instead of salted vegetable stock). Taste and adjust if necessary. Keep warm, or reheat on low heat at serving time.

While the dahl is cooking, choose one or more vegetables and their cooking methods from the list below. For 4 people, assuming you serve the dahl with rice or naan, you will need 6-8 big handfuls of raw vegetables, much more if you use spinach or kale.

Roasting:

Toss the vegetable(s) in sunflower oil, sprinkle lightly with salt and cumin seeds and roast in a pre-heated oven.

Aubergine, cubed, 30-40 min at 200 C (400 F) static/180 C (350 F) fan/gas 6 until very soft
Courgette, thickly sliced, 20 min at 220 C (425 F) static/200 C (400 F) fan/gas 7
Peppers, cut into big chunks, 20-30 min at 200 C (400 F) static/180 C (350 F) fan/gas 6

Cauliflower, cut into florets, 30 min at 220 C (425 F) static/200 C (400 F) fan/gas 7

Sweet potato, scrubbed and diced, peel left on! 30 min at 220 C (425 F) static/200 C (400 F) fan/gas 7

Squash or pumpkin, diced, 20-30 min at 220 C (425 F) static/200 C (400 F) fan/gas 7

Parsnips, cut into sticks, parboil in water for 1 min, roast 20-30 min at 220 C (425 F) static/200 C (400 F) fan/gas 7

Beetroot, peeled and cut into 2 cm dice, 30 min at 220 C (425 F) static/200 C (400 F) fan/gas 7

Frying:

Stir-fry in vegetable oil: the process is short for spinach, and takes a bit longer for tougher vegetables like cabbage or peppers. Add some salt at the end.

> *Kale, 1 large bag*
> *Spinach, 1 large bag*
> *White or green cabbage, ¼-½ shredded*
> *Peppers, roughly chopped*
> *Onions, sliced*
> *Leek, sliced*
> *Courgettes, sliced*

Boiling/steaming:

For boiling, add 1 tsp salt to the water. Bring to the boil. Add the vegetables and cook for the required time (cooking time is from the moment the water has reached boiling point again!). Drain before serving.

Steaming: use a steamer, or steam the vegetables in 1-cm-deep water in a pan.

Broccoli or cauliflower, in small florets, 1-2 min boiling, 5-7 min steaming.

Carrots, sliced, 5 mins boiling, 10-14 min steaming.

French beans or runner beans, 5 min boiling.

Beetroot, boiled whole with peel for 30-60 min, depending on size. To serve, peel and dice.

For your big feast with friends: choose a large variety from above and serve with plenty of chutneys, rice, naan and salads. Carrot and seed salad (page 56), cucumber salad with yoghurt and garlic dressing (page 56) and crunchy Vietnamese style salad (page 65) would go well.

Broccoli and roast squash cheesecake (optionally GF)

I am a bit of a baked cheesecake fan – the creaminess of the filling in contrast to the crunch of the base is just heavenly. Enjoying savoury food much more than sweet, I was totally hooked when first eating a crab cheesecake at The Ninth Wave restaurant on Mull.

This is my vegetarian take on it –- a beautiful recipe for a night of entertaining friends. Here, I am adding roast butternut squash and broccoli to the filling. Other vegetables such as roast peppers, roast baby courgettes, steamed asparagus, peas and stir-fried leeks make a great filling too.

Serve with a tomato salsa (page 68) or tomato and chilli sauce (page 94), some roast potato wedges and other salads on the side.

Serves 4
Pastry:
140 g wholemeal or plain flour (or GF plain flour)
70 g cold salted butter
Cold water

Place flour into a bowl. Dice the cold butter finely and add to the bowl. Using your fingertips, work the fat into the flour until it all resembles fine breadcrumbs.

Add just enough water, about 1-2 tsp, to form a smooth dough. Do not knead. Place pastry into a tub, cover and leave in a cool place to rest for 1 hour.

Preheat the oven to 200 C (400 F) static/180 C (350 F) fan/gas 6.

After the pastry has rested, line a 20 cm round cake tin or pie dish with baking parchment, enough of it to overhang the edge.

Roll out the pastry on a floured surface to about ½ cm thickness or just press it into the dish with your hands. It will only cover the base – while pastry is delicious, I try to minimise the use of it due to its high fat content, especially in a recipe that also includes lots of cheese!

Cover the pastry with a sheet of baking parchment and weigh this down with blind baking lentils or two teaspoons to keep the paper in place.

Put the tin into the preheated oven and blind bake the crust for 30 minutes (longer if using a ceramic pie dish) until the pastry is firm to the touch.

Take out, remove lentils/spoons and top layer of baking paper. Leave the oven on.

Filling:
Vegetables for roasting:
300 g butternut squash, peeled weight
100 g broccoli
4 cloves of garlic
Olive oil

400 g cream cheese
40 g Stilton or similar blue cheese, or Parmesan cheese
2 large eggs
1 lightly heaped dessertspoon cornflour
½ tsp salt

Start on making the filling while the pastry rests, and later gets blind baked.

Preheat the oven to 200 C (400 F) static/180 C (350 F) fan/gas 6 if not already done for the pastry.

Prepare the vegetables: Peel the butternut squash and cut into 1 cm dice. Chop the garlic finely. Place both into an ovenproof dish, add 1 tbsp olive oil and ½ tsp salt and toss until well coated.

Place into the preheated oven and roast until cooked through and slightly browned at the edges – this will take 20-30 minutes. Put aside.

Cut the broccoli into very small florets. Place into a small saucepan with a fitting lid (or use your steamer). Add 1 cm water to the pan, bring to boil, and steam, with the lid on, for 3 minutes. Drain immediately and leave to cool.

Place cream cheese and broken up/grated Stilton or other cheese into a mixing bowl, and using an electric hand mixer, whisk for 1-2 minutes until well combined and fluffed up. Now add the eggs, cornflour and ½ tsp of salt, and mix to combine.

Once the roast squash and broccoli have cooled a bit, add them to the cheese mix and fold in.

Get the dish with the blind-baked pastry, pour the filling on top of the base, and smooth the top.

Place into the oven, turning it down to 170 C (340 F) static/150 C (300 F) fan/gas 4.

Bake for 50 minutes to 1 hour until the filling has set.

Leave to rest for 15 minutes in a warm place before lifting out of the baking dish. The cheesecake can be served warm (now!), or left to cool and eaten at room temperature – it's great for a summer picnic. If you want to use it the next day, store in the fridge once cooled, and make sure to take it out at least 1 hour before eating.

Fish and Seafood

Industrialised fishing has purged our oceans of so much life – overfishing and by-catch have depleted stocks at such a rate that there is no time for them to regenerate. While this is very bad news for the ocean as a system, it also affects millions of people for whom fish is an important source of protein, and whose livelihood depends on it. To protect our oceans, and make sure that future generations will still have fish to catch, sourcing sustainably caught fish should be not only a choice, but a must. Look out for the blue MSC (Marine Stewardship Council) label for ocean catch, or for ASC (Aquaculture Stewardship Council) certified farmed seafood. Speak with your fishmonger to make sure the catch comes from sustainable fisheries.

If you live or holiday by the coast, talk with the fishers and buy directly from fishing vessels that use handline, jig, pole and line, spear or harpoon, rod and line, bottom long line, drift net, or pots and creels, or dive for shellfish. These methods are seen by the Marine Conservation Society as sustainable.

When I started writing this book, it included three recipes for mackerel, which then was still thought plentiful. Unfortunately, as of March 2019 the Marine Stewardship Council has declared mackerel from North East Atlantic fisheries as no longer sustainable due to years of overfishing – you will not find this fish with an MSC label in British shops any more.

My stepson, who is a local fisherman, works single-handed and fishes sustainably, using handlines to catch pollack, and pots for lobster and crab. We source most of our fish from him.

Baked pollack with ginger (GF, DF)

Pollack belongs to the same family as cod and haddock – the flesh is just not as white as that of its cousins, and it has never been much appreciated by buyers. However, it tastes great and hasn't been overfished. You can use other white fish for the recipe (haddock, cod, sole), but also salmon or freshwater fish like trout and carp are very tasty cooked this way.

> Serves 4
> 4 fillets of pollack (about 700-800 g in total weight)
> 1½ tbsp toasted sesame oil
> Juice of 1 lime
> Juice of ½ lemon
> 1 dessertspoon honey – runny, or melted gently over heat
> 2 tbsp soya sauce or 1½ tbsp tamari sauce
> 125 ml dry white wine or 115 ml water and 2 tsp white wine vinegar
> 1 chunky 2-cm-long piece of ginger
> Optional: finely chopped chilli or chilli flakes

Preheat the oven to 200 C (400 F) static/180 C (350 F) fan/gas 6.

Wash the fish in cold water, pat dry with kitchen paper and place into an ovenproof dish.

Make up the sauce: Grate the ginger finely (I usually wash it and leave the skin on) and mix with oil, the citrus juices, honey, soya sauce and wine.

Pour over the fillets – make sure ginger is evenly distributed. Sprinkle with chilli if wanted.

Place, uncovered, in the preheated oven and bake for 12-18 minutes. (Touched gently, the fish should flake apart. Cooking time depends on the thickness of the fillets, but also on the dish you use – ceramic will take longer to heat than metal.)

Serve with brown rice or rice noodles and stir-fried or steamed greens like pak choi, broccoli or kale.

Creamy smoked haddock, leek and potato stew
(GF, optionally DF)

This is something between a soup and a stew; however, because of its richness, it makes a very filling dinner if served with chunky bread and a crunchy salad like celeriac and wholegrain mustard slaw (see page 52).

Make sure the haddock you buy is MSC approved. The recipe will work with any smoked white fish.

> Serves 4 as a wholesome meal, 6 if served as a soup
> 1 small white onion
> 1 tbsp butter or sunflower oil
> 2 leeks with plenty of fresh green leaves, washed well
> 1.2 ltr fish stock
> Zest of 1 washed unwaxed lemon
> 1 bay leaf
> 4 large, white-skinned, floury potatoes, about 800-900 g
> 4 large smoked haddock fillets (about 600 g total weight)
> Salt and pepper
> 150 ml double cream or vegan alternative

Chop the onion very finely and fry in butter or oil on a medium heat until translucent but not browned, stirring regularly. Halve the leek lengthways and slice very finely, including all the green leaves which will give the stew its great highlights of green but are also very nutritious. Cook for 1 minute until wilted. Add the fish stock, bay leaf and grated zest of lemon. Cover the pan with a lid. While this comes to a boil, scrub the potatoes (I would leave the skin on if they are white potatoes), dice finely and put into the pan too.

Once the mix comes to the boil, set a timer for 10 minutes. This should be enough to soften the potatoes.

Take out the bay leaf. Using a soup blender, whizz part of the mix, but make sure there are still plenty of potato chunks left. If using a kitchen processor for this, just take out about ⅓, blend, then return to the pan.

Keeping the stew on a very low simmer, now add the fish fillets and poach them for 5-7 minutes until cooked through. If they still have their skins attached, carefully take the fillets out of the pan, leave to cool slightly, then remove the skin before returning the fish to the pan.

Add the cream, ½ tsp salt and some ground black pepper, and stir through. While doing this, break up the fish into large-ish chunks. Taste and adjust seasoning if necessary. Heat through until almost boiling, then serve right away.

Matjes herring in a creamy marinade with gherkins and apple (GF, optionally DF)

I remember this being one of the dishes that grew on me the older I got – my granny used to make it every fortnight or so, bringing back salted whole herring from the shop, soaking them for two days to wash out the salt, and then serving them in a creamy marinade with boiled potatoes on the side.

I am not even sure whether it's possible to obtain whole salted herring these days. I use matjes herring instead – fillets of fish, lightly salted and then sold vacuum-packed in sunflower oil. It's a German/Dutch speciality, and thanks to the large Polish community in Britain who love matjes too, it can be bought in most large supermarkets these days.

Replace the sour cream with dairy free yoghurt and dairy free cream alternative if you need to avoid dairy.

Serve with boiled or baked potatoes, or as part of a big salad selection, with freshly made bread – rye will be especially suitable.

> Serves 2 for a main course, 4 as a side
> *1 400 g pack matjes fillets*
>
> *Marinade:*
> *3 tbsp sour cream (or 2 heaped tbsp Greek-style yoghurt and 1 tbsp double cream)*
> *1 bay leaf*
> *4 gherkins*
> *½ large dessert apple*
> *1 small white onion*
> *1-2 tbsp gherkin liquid*
> *Freshly ground pepper*
> *Salt – to taste*

Place the matjes into a bowl of cold water, cover and leave in the fridge overnight to get rid of some of the salt – sometimes the fillets can be quite salty.

The next day, drain the fish, pat dry with a kitchen towel, then cut each into 3 pieces.

Make up the marinade in a bowl: put in sour cream (or yoghurt and double cream), sliced gherkins, very finely chopped onion (it will taste good without, so if you struggle with raw onion just omit it), finely diced apple (skin on), the bay leaf, some liquid from the gherkin jar and pepper. Stir well, and add the fish and fold in. Leave in a cool place for at least one hour (for flavours to mingle, it's best to leave it for 2-3 hours), then remove bay leaf, stir gently, taste and add salt and more gherkin liquid if necessary. Serve at room temperature.

The dish will keep in the fridge for up to three days, though I find it tastes best on the day you made it.

Mussels cooked in cider and leeks, served with lovage

One of my favourite 'mussel memories' is sharing the task of cleaning and preparing, and later eating, 5 kg of mussels at a friend's birthday party over glasses of prosecco, chat and laughter.

Often seen as a bit 'fiddly' because of the debearding aspect, mussels actually make for a very quick meal – if you cook them for your family!

While we usually do not serve mussels to an Abbey full of guests (cleaning 30 kg of them would be quite a task), I wanted to have one recipe in this book.

These bivalves are not only tasty and nutritious, they are also one of the farmed seafoods which has very little impact on the environment. To 'grow' mussels, ropes are suspended from buoys and left for a year for them to attach themselves and increase in size. No extra feed is needed, and escapees are not a threat to other wild mussels or other species.

Inverlussa Mussel Farm on Mull, just a few miles out of Craignure on your way to Fionnphort, offers fresh mussels for sale on an honesty box basis – we rarely drive by without stopping.

We ate mussels prepared as described below at the above-mentioned birthday party. It's Pamela Brunton's recipe, a talented chef who now owns, with her partner Rob, the successful restaurant 'Inver' on the shores of Loch Fyne.

> Serves 4 for a main course and 6 for starters
> 2 kg mussels
> 1 tbsp butter or sunflower oil
> 1 medium-sized leek
> 1 clove of garlic
> 250 ml dry cider
> 2 tbsp chopped lovage, or if not at hand,
> 2 tbsp chopped parsley and 2 tbsp chopped celery leaves

Clean the mussels in the kitchen sink, pulling off the 'beard', the threadlike fibres with which the mussels attach themselves to rocks (or ropes), and any big barnacles which have taken up residence on their shells.

Discard any mussels that are broken, or do not close when tapped gently on a surface.

Rinse with fresh water. Put aside.

Prepare your vegetables: clean the leek under cold fresh water, and slice finely. Mince the garlic finely.

In a very large heavy-based pan, fry the leeks gently in butter or oil over a medium heat until just softened. Add the garlic and cider, increase the heat to high, bring to boil and cook until reduced by half.

Now add the mussels, and cover the pan with the lid. Wait for the liquid in the pan to come back to the boil – you will hear it bubbling and see steam escaping from under the lid. Set timer to cook for 2 minutes, then stir through with a wooden spoon to move some of the top layer into the bottom. Cover again and cook for another minute or two until the mussels have opened up and slightly firmed up.

Add the lovage, or parsley and celery (the strong flavour of lovage reminds one of celery and parsley – that's why they make good substitutes), and stir through.

Serve with roast potato wedges or fresh bread and some dry cider on the side.

Meat

There exists a very strong connection between humans and land here on the island. It's especially noticeable in people who work the fields and hills. Whether a farm or croft has been in a family for generations, or has been taken over by incomers, their love and care for the land, and the animals who feed on it, is reflected in the ways they look after it daily.

At the Abbey we serve meat once or twice a week. Lamb, beef and pork are sourced, if possible, on Iona; if not, then from Mull. This way we support the local farmers and crofters who raise their animals in a sustainable way, and the slaughterhouse on Mull.

Lamb, bacon and vegetable casserole (GF, DF)

This is a heart-warming stew with its melt-in-the-mouth pieces of lamb in a rich chunky sauce. If you can, buy a whole shoulder of lamb rather than already diced – that way you can keep the pieces big and chunky.

Curiously, meat imported from New Zealand is often cheaper than British lamb, but try to buy local to support our farmers, even if that means not being able to eat it for a few months due to its seasonality.

Here on Iona, farmers also sell hogget, the meat of a lamb aged between one and two – depending on when the animals are taken to slaughter. Hogget is available all year round, and is just as tasty as young lamb.

This dish will feed up to 8 people – if you have a few more guests just add a tin of cooked butter beans.

Serves 8
1 shoulder of lamb or hogget, boned (about 1.5 kg weight) or 1.5 kg diced
*   shoulder, if whole is not available*
2 medium-sized onions
4 cloves of garlic
3 sticks of celery, washed
3 small to medium-sized carrots, scrubbed or peeled
300 g smoked bacon
300 ml white wine
2 tsp thyme
2 tsp rosemary
2 bay leaves
1 tbsp tomato puree
1 400 g tin chopped tomatoes

I prefer starting this dish off on the cooker top and finishing it in the oven; however you can cook the stew solely on the hob if preferred.

First, prepare your ingredients: Cut the meat into 4 cm cubes, trim off excess fat. Put aside.

Cut the bacon into short 1-cm-wide strips.

Chop onions and garlic finely. Slice the celery and carrots.

Preheat your oven: if you have a choice, go for a static oven, as a fan will dry out the stew more quickly and you will have to keep an eye out and replenish liquid during cooking: 150 C (300 F) static/130 C (265 F) fan/gas 2-3.

Use an ovenproof cast iron casserole dish with a close-fitting lid or similar. Heat up on medium heat for 2 minutes, then lower one third of the lamb pieces into it. The pieces should start to sear and sizzle immediately. Do not use oil at this point as lamb tends to be fatty anyway and the frying releases this, so the meat can cook in it. Leave the pieces to fry on one side for 1-2 minutes (they will stick first, but will come loose more easily once browned) before stirring to brown all other sides. This process will take a wee while but is important if you want to achieve a deeply flavoured and dark-coloured sauce.

When the first batch of meat is browned all over, scoop it out and repeat with the rest of the meat in two further batches.

After this, pour the released lamb fat into a bowl lined with aluminium foil – in there the fat can set before being thrown out in the general waste. Do not pour down the drain!

Using the same casserole (don't wash it) fry the onions and garlic in 2 tbsp of olive oil on a medium heat until transparent. Add carrots and celery and sweat for a while with the lid on before adding the bacon.

When the latter is cooked, add the herbs and pour in the glass of wine. Using your wooden spoon scrape the base of the pan to stir any of the residue left from frying the meat – this will give your stew colour and flavour.

Add the lamb, tomato puree, chopped tomatoes and about 400 ml of cold water – the meat should be almost covered by the liquid. If not, add a bit more.

Get a piece of baking parchment of similar size to the diameter of your cooking vessel. Scrunch it up, then unfold and place right on top of the stew - this will help keep the moisture in during the long cooking process.

Cover with a lid and bring to the boil. After 5 minutes' further cooking on the hob, move the casserole carefully into the preheated oven. Set a timer for 3 hrs – if you use the fan setting of your electric oven, check after 1.5 hrs whether there is enough liquid covering the meat and add more hot water from the kettle if not.

After the 3 hours the meat should be very tender – but if it is not, just cook it for another 30 minutes.

The dish is now ready to be served, or can be cooled and heated later for 45-55 min at 180 C (350 F) static/160 C (325 F) fan/gas 4.

Remove the bay leaves, then stir in some freshly ground pepper before serving – I tend not to add salt as the bacon releases plenty of it.

Lovely with mashed or roast potatoes, serve this dish with a good helping of greens like broccoli or kale.

Venison ragu (GF, optionally DF)

While a Bolognese sauce made with beef mince is a trusted favourite at the Abbey, this version which we make with venison, sourced from our neighbouring island of Mull, is even richer in taste and makes a beautiful sauce to serve with pasta or in a hunter's pie. This recipe does not use garlic or any herbs other than bay leaves – which in the Italian cooking tradition is quite normal.

> **Serves 3 in a mash-covered pie, 4 as a sauce for pasta**
> *1 tbsp sunflower oil*
> *500 g minced venison (or beef mince)*
> *4 rashers of bacon, diced finely*
> *1 tbsp olive oil*
> *1 small onion, finely chopped*
> *1½ large sticks of celery, very finely diced*
> *1 medium carrot, very finely diced*
> *1 bay leaf*
> *150 ml red wine*
> *1 heaped tbsp tomato puree*
> *½ tsp salt*
> *Water*
> *100 ml milk (or dairy free alternative)*

Heat up a heavy-based pan for 2 min on a medium heat, then add the minced venison and fry until browned and fallen apart. Add the bacon, and cook for a further minute, stirring all the time.

Scrape the meat into a bowl and put aside. Place the pan (do not wash it) back on the heat, add 1 tbsp olive oil and all the vegetables. Sauté these on a low to medium heat until softened but not browned.

Increase the heat again, add the wine (or the same amount of water), and using your wooden spoon scrape any residue left from frying the meat off the base of the pan. Add bay leaf, tomato puree, meat and salt, then add more water to barely cover the meat. Stir through, cover with a lid, and bring back to the boil.

Once bubbling, turn the heat down to very low and leave the sauce to simmer for at least 2 hours – I prefer even longer: at home I might start cooking mid-morning and leave it simmering slowly for the whole day. Make sure to set a timer every hour to remind you to check on it. If it becomes too thick and starts catching on the bottom, add more hot water.

After the main cooking time, add the milk (omit if you want to keep it dairy free) and continue to simmer for a further 40-50 minutes. Before serving, remove the bay leaf, add some freshly ground pepper and taste to see if it needs a bit more salt. The sauce should have a pretty thick consistency, so if it's on the runny side, cook it on a high heat for a few minutes, while stirring all time, to evaporate some of the liquid.

Serve on a bed of spaghetti, tagliatelle or similar. This sauce is also good as a pizza topping (in case you have leftovers) or covered with mashed potatoes and baked in the oven à la 'hunter's pie'.

Italian-style pork meatballs (GF, DF)

A recipe given to me by Angela Gosetti, who herself is a great cook. Her Italian husband taught her to make these. We have added a few more herbs (and left out the white wine).

Wonderfully aromatic, they are great as part of a buffet, but really we like serving them on pasta tossed in olive oil and garlic, or with our rich tomato sauce (page 73).

> Serves 4 for a main course, or 6 for starters
>
> *500 g pork mince – try not to use very lean mince, as the fat carries the flavour and also keeps the meatballs moist. Most of it will run off during roasting anyway, which makes the dish less fatty.*
>
> *1 lightly heaped tsp fennel seeds*
> *1 good pinch, or more if you like it spicy, of chilli flakes*
> *1 level tsp sea salt*
> *2 cloves of garlic, finely minced*
> *A good pinch each of dried basil, oregano and rosemary*
> *½ tsp freshly ground pepper*

Do the following well before roasting the meatballs to give the meat time to marinate in the spices: Place pork mince, spices, herbs, salt and pepper into a bowl and mix until well combined. Shape golf-ball-sized meatballs, and place into a roasting dish. Cover and leave to marinate for at least one hour in the fridge or a cool place.

You can pan-fry these for 10-15 minutes in some sunflower oil. In the Abbey, pan-frying being too laborious for the amount of guests, we roast them instead: Preheat the oven to 240 C (475 F) static/220 C (425 F) fan/gas 9.

Place the meatballs into the hot oven and roast for 10 minutes (longer if you use a ceramic dish, which needs more time to heat up).

Serve immediately on their own as a tapas-style starter, or on top of pasta tossed in olive oil or tomato sauce, sprinkled with parmesan.

You could also make burgers out of the mix and grill them on your BBQ – they are great on a roll with some sliced tomatoes.

Keema matar – curried mince with peas (GF, DF)

This is my version of the famous Indian meat dish. A great curry to have the traditional way, with rice or naan and a big salad, but it's also good as the filling for a cottage pie, the mashed potatoes spiced with some nutmeg and turmeric.

The hands-on cooking process is really quick – the time demand lies, as for any good stew, in the duration the meat has to simmer. The longer, the better!

Serves 4
500 g beef or lean lamb mince
1 large onion, finely chopped
Sunflower oil
1 chunky 2 cm piece of root ginger
½ tsp chilli flakes
2 tsp ground cumin
1 level tsp ground turmeric
3 tsp ground coriander
1 tsp ground cardamom
½ tsp ground cinnamon
½ tsp ground nutmeg
½ tsp ground cloves
½ tsp soft brown sugar
1 x 400 g tin chopped tomatoes
200 g frozen peas
Salt and pepper
Roughly chopped fresh coriander to serve

Heat up a heavy-based pan on a medium heat – use sunflower oil for frying if using beef mince; lamb is usually fatty enough to fry well without any added oil. Once hot, add the mince and fry until browned. Add the onions and ginger and keep on stir-frying for 2-3 minutes until the onions become translucent.

Add all the spices, sugar and chopped tomatoes. Fill the tomato tin with fresh cold water ¾ way up and add this to the dish. Season with 1 level tsp of salt. Cover with a lid and bring to the boil on a high heat. Once boiling, turn it down to a low simmer and cook for at least 2 hours, stirring from time to time.

After this, add the peas, bring back to the boil and simmer for 5 minutes on low heat. The dish is now ready to eat with your favourite sides. It freezes well and will taste just as good as a leftover, if not better!

Vegetable Side Dishes

Slow-cooked turnip (swede) with wholegrain mustard and pumpkin seeds (GF, optionally VEGAN)

Swedes and turnips belong to the same family: what many people call a swede is really a Swedish turnip. Therefore, in Scotland, we often call them turnips.

Whatever you like to call the large, hardy, orange-fleshed vegetable, it is still seen, by some people, as a second-best food: something that had to be eaten after the war because there was nothing much else.

How wrong! It's a beautiful-tasting root once roasted or slow-cooked, with earthy sweetness and a nutty taste. Whether as a trusted companion to haggis (when it might be called 'neeps'), in a rich vegetable or meat stew or as a side to your Sunday roast, it has every right to be part of today's diet.

Serves 4
1 medium-sized Swedish turnip
Butter or olive oil
1 level tsp salt
½ tsp freshly ground pepper
2 tsp wholegrain mustard (check that it's free of gluten if that is an issue)
100 ml double cream or any dairy free alternative to cream
3 tbsp pumpkin seeds

Peel the turnip and cut into 1 cm dice. Place, together with 1 tbsp butter or oil, into a heavy-based pan. Cover with a lid and heat slowly on a medium heat. Once it starts sizzling, give it a stir and turn down heat to almost the lowest setting, cooking the vegetable covered for 20-30 minutes until very soft. You might have to experiment with the heat – your lowest setting might be just too low, so increase accordingly: you want to cook the turnip without browning it. While this happens, place the pumpkin seeds into a small pan and toast (without any additional oil) on a medium heat until lightly browned and fragrant – do not leave the pan unattended.

Once the turnip is very soft and golden orange, add salt, pepper, mustard and cream and heat through.

Serve with the toasted pumpkin seeds sprinkled on top.

Savoy cabbage with cumin, tamari and lemon
(GF, VEGAN)

This recipe uses Savoy cabbage with its beautifully dark blistered leaves – however, a sweetheart variety or even a plain white cabbage will taste good prepared this way.

Serves 4-6
1 medium-sized Savoy cabbage
1 clove of garlic, minced
1 tsp cumin seeds (or 1 level tsp ground cumin)
1 tbsp sesame oil (or sunflower oil)
1 dessertspoon tamari sauce (or soya sauce)
Juice of ½ lemon

Discard any withered or browned leaves of the cabbage. Cut out the hard centre stalk and wash the leaves in a sink of cold water. Leave to drain well or spin dry in a salad spinner – any water left in the pockets of the cabbage leaves will make the dish watery.

Chop into shreds. Heat up the oil together with the cumin seeds (if using ground cumin, add with the cabbage, not now) in a suitable heavy-based pan. When hot, add the cabbage and garlic. Stir-fry on a high heat until some bits are browned, and the pieces are halfway cooked through but still have plenty of bite.

Take off the heat, add lemon juice and tamari sauce, stir through and serve immediately.

Braised carrots with lemon and thyme (GF, optionally VEGAN)

The slow cooking of the carrots brings out their sweetness – don't rush the process.

Serves 4
4 large carrots
Butter or olive oil
½ tsp dried thyme
Zest of ½ unwaxed lemon
Juice of ½ lemon
½ tsp salt
½ tsp freshly ground pepper

Scrub or peel the carrots and slice or dice. Place into a heavy-based pan together with 1 level tbsp butter or olive oil, thyme and lemon zest. Cover and heat up on a medium heat until sizzling. Stir, cover again, turn heat down to low and cook without browning until tender – this will take 15-25 minutes. Adjust heat if necessary – sometimes 'low' is just not hot enough …

Add lemon juice, salt and pepper, serve.

Slow-cooked red cabbage (GF, DF)

A German favourite, in Saxony anyway – delicious with a roast, whether that's a nut loaf or roast beef.

I tend to make a large amount and freeze half of it to use another time.

> Serves 6-8
> *1 small red cabbage*
> *1 large onion*
> *1 large cooking apple (or 2 dessert apples)*
> *Sunflower oil*
> *⅓ tsp ground cloves (or 4 whole cloves)*
> *1 large bay leaf*
> *½ cup of water*
> *optional: ½ glass of red wine*
> *1 dessertspoon soft brown sugar*
> *2-3 dessertspoons of apple cider vinegar (or other vinegar)*
> *Salt*

Take the first layer of leaves off the cabbage and discard. Cut remaining cabbage in half, discard the hard stalk, then shred finely, with a knife or mandoline grater.

Peel, halve and slice the onion finely. Peel, core and dice the apple.

Heat up the oil in a heavy-based pan. Add onions and fry until transparent without browning. Add cabbage and apple, stir-fry for 5 minutes on a medium to high heat, then add cloves, bay leaf, water, red wine if using, sugar and vinegar. Cover with a lid, bring to a boil, then turn heat down to low and simmer for 30-40 minutes, stirring from time to time and checking that there is enough liquid in the bottom so it doesn't burn.

After it is cooked, remove bay leaf and add ½ to 1 tsp of salt. Taste, and add more sugar or vinegar to your liking.

Sweet Treats

Orange and cardamom muffins (GF)

One wouldn't know these muffins are gluten free – the addition of yoghurt and almonds makes them moist and light. They keep well for days in an airtight container without going dry.

Toast and grind the cardamom seeds yourself for the best flavour. However, the ground cardamom bought in a shop will work – you might just want to add a bit more …

To be exact with the measurements, I find it easier to measure the liquids on electronic scales rather than in a jug.

Makes 12
280 g plain gluten free flour
2 tsp baking powder (gluten free)
1 tsp bicarbonate of soda
1 tsp freshly ground cardamom (or 1½-2 tsp if shop-bought ground spice)
80 g ground almonds
½ tsp salt
150 g caster sugar
130 ml olive oil
140 ml milk
140 ml Greek-style yoghurt
2 eggs
Zest of 1 medium-sized orange (washed well before grating)
Juice of half a lemon

Preheat the oven to 200 C (400 F) static/180 C (350 F) fan/gas 6. Line a muffin tray with 12 cases.

Mix all the dry ingredients in a bowl and quickly whisk through with a hand whisk to combine and break up any lumps.

Place olive oil, milk, yoghurt, eggs, orange zest and lemon juice into a jug and mix with a whisk until well combined.

Add the liquid to the bowl of dry ingredients and fold in until just combined. Fill the cases and bake for 17–20 minutes until a skewer inserted in one muffin comes out clean. Leave to cool a little before eating.

Sticky toffee pudding (optionally DF and GF)

I fell in love with this the first time I had it. Is there anything more beautiful and heart-warming (in a pudding sense) than buttery toffee sauce?

Serves 8-10
For the cake:
100 g of chopped (pitted) dates
125 ml water
½ tsp bicarbonate of soda
50 g salted butter (or dairy free spread and a good pinch of salt)
55 g caster sugar
1 free range egg
1 tsp vanilla essence
105 g self-raising flour (wheat or gluten free)

For the sauce:
65 g soft brown sugar
50 ml double cream
50 g salted butter

To make a dairy free alternative to the above sauce, cook together
7 tbsp soft or dark brown sugar
150 ml coconut milk
¼ tsp vanilla extract
A pinch of salt

Preheat the oven to 180 C (350 F) static/160 C (325 F) fan/gas 4-5. Oil a small cake tin – something around the size of 18 cm diameter or length.

Put dates and water in a pan, bring to boil. Remove from heat and stir in the soda. Leave to cool in a sink filled with cold water halfway up the pan.

In a bowl beat butter and sugar together with an electric whisk on high speed, until pale and creamy. Add the egg and vanilla essence.

Putting the electric mixer aside, add the cooled dates and mix in with a spatula or spoon. Sieve the flour into the bowl, then fold it into the butter mix with large movements, trying not to over-beat it.

Turn mixture into the prepared tin. Bake in the oven for 25-35 min or until a skewer inserted into the centre of the cake comes out clean.

To make the sauce, put all ingredients into a pan and bring slowly to the boil. Simmer on low heat for 1 minute.

Serve immediately with cream or plain yoghurt (we prefer the latter as the sourness of the yoghurt is a good balance to the heavy sweetness), or serve later, heating up the cake for 5-10 min in a warm oven (140 C) sprinkled lightly with some water beforehand to avoid drying it out.

Chocolate puddle pudding with orange and cardamom (optionally GF and DF)

Another Abbey favourite – I inherited the recipe when starting to work as the cook. I have since added some orange zest and cardamom to the mix, which makes it taste a bit more exotic. Leave these out if you want the original flavour. Best eaten freshly baked from the oven!

Serves 4

First make the sauce:
90 g soft brown sugar
25 g cocoa powder (not drinking chocolate)
200 ml hot water from the kettle

Mix all the above ingredients together in a jug or bowl. Set aside.

Preheat oven to 180 C (350 F) static/160 C (325 F) fan/gas 4-5.

Grease a 16 cm diameter/length deep (leakproof) baking tin or ovenproof dish.

For the cake
90 g salted butter (or dairy free spread and a good pinch of salt)
90 g caster sugar
Zest of one medium large washed orange
½ tsp of freshly ground cardamom seeds (slightly more if already ground)
2 eggs
1 tsp vanilla essence
25 g cocoa (not drinking chocolate)
90 g self-raising flour (wheat or gluten free)

Cream butter and sugar with an electric whisk on highest speed for 2 minutes until pale and creamy. Add eggs, one by one, then the vanilla essence, orange zest and cardamom, while mixing. Put the mixer aside.

Sieve flour and cocoa into the bowl, then fold into the mix with big movements, using a spatula or spoon, until just combined. Turn into the prepared tin.

Pour the chocolate sauce over the sponge mix, put into the oven and bake for 20-25 minutes or until a skewer comes out clean.

Serve immediately with yoghurt, ice cream or cream.

Though best served straight from the oven, if you would like to pre-make it and reheat it later, use only half of the sauce for baking, and reheat for 10 minutes in a preheated oven at 150 C (300 F) static/130 C (265 F) fan/gas 2 with the rest of the sauce poured over it.

Chocolate crumble cheesecake (optionally GF)

A baked cheesecake available in most bakeries in Germany – beautifully rich, perfect with its different textures: a crunchy base and crumbles, and the soft creamy filling. The original German recipe uses quark, the high fat (40%) variety which is not available here. We use cream cheese instead, which produces a very similar result.

> Serves 8
> *First make the pastry and crumble mix*
> *80 g plain flour (wheat or gluten free)*
> *40 g butter*
> *40 g soft brown sugar*
> *18 g cocoa powder (not drinking chocolate)*
> *½ egg*
> *½ tsp baking powder*

Preheat the oven to 170 C (340 F) static/150 C (300 F) fan/gas 3-4. Grease and paper-line an 18 or 20 cm round cake tin.

Place cool butter, chopped into small dice, sugar, flour, baking powder and cocoa into a mixing bowl and work the fat into the dry mix by hand, until it resembles breadcrumbs. In a mug, whisk the egg by hand before adding about half of it to the crumble mix (you will add the other half to the cream cheese). Form the crumbles into a lump of pastry. DO NOT knead this or the pastry and crumbles will lose their lightness.

Reserve a third of the mix in the bowl and use the other two-thirds to line the prepared baking tray. Roll out the lump of pastry on a floured surface to a sheet of about ½ cm thickness. Place this into the dish and press up to line it halfway up the sides too. Put aside.

> *Make the cheese filling:*
> *350 g full fat cream cheese*
> *100 g caster sugar*
> *2½ medium-sized eggs*
> *1 dessertspoon custard powder or cornflour*
> *1 tsp vanilla essence*

Place cream cheese and sugar into a bowl and mix with an electric whisk until fluffy. Add the eggs, one by one, while still mixing. Finally put in vanilla essence and custard powder and combine. Pour the cheese filling into the cake tin lined with the pastry base. Tear the leftover chunk of pastry into marble-sized pieces and scatter these all over the cheese mix.

Put into the preheated oven and bake for about an hour or longer – the filling should be just set in the middle, so slightly wobbly to the touch, the cheese mix not too browned.

Leave to cool fully before turning it out, peeling off the paper and placing it on a serving dish.

This cake is almost better the next day. Keep in the fridge but take it out at least one hour before serving so it has a chance to come to room temperature.

Orange and almond cake (GF, DF)

Naturally free of gluten and dairy, this dessert came to the Abbey kitchen with a volunteer from Australia. Using whole oranges gives the cake a slight and pleasing bitterness.

You will need a food processor or jug blender for this.

Serves 6-8
1 medium orange
3 eggs
100 g ground almonds
1 tbsp of fine polenta or cornflour
80 g soft brown sugar
½ tsp baking powder

First, place the orange into a small, tall pan, cover with water and boil for 1 hour until soft. Drain and leave to cool a bit. This can be done the day before.

Preheat the oven to 180 C (350 F) static/160 C (325 F) fan/gas 4-5.

Grease and bottom-line with baking parchment an 18 or 20 cm diameter round cake tin.

Roughly cut up the orange (pick out any pips you can find), place into a food processor (peel and all) and whiz to a fine puree.

Into a bowl, place eggs and sugar, and whisk using an electric whisk on high speed for about 5 minutes, until the mixture has about tripled in size and is all foamy.

Place almonds and polenta into a different vessel, sieve baking powder into it, then stir through with a hand whisk, breaking up any lumps in the almonds.

Fold the orange puree into the foamy egg mix by hand, using big slow movements to keep the air in it, then add the dry ingredients and keep on folding gently.

Turn into the prepared tin and bake for 30-40 minutes or until a skewer comes out clean. Leave to cool fully before removing from the tin.

This tastes excellent with some thick yoghurt (dairy free or not) or crème fraiche and, if you have them, fresh raspberries on the side.

Fruit crumble cake (optionally DF)

Another German favourite – in my family we often make it with sweet yeast dough for the base; others will use a mix which is somewhere between a 'dense' sponge and a soft pastry, as in the recipe below.

It's one of those wonderful base recipes which you can adapt to your heart's content, using whatever fruit is in season. Just make sure to have some breadcrumbs (home-made or panko style) ready for very juicy fruit such as gooseberries or rhubarb (which, by the way, is classed as a vegetable).

This cake makes a great pudding when still slightly warm, served with custard, or a delicious treat for afternoon tea, with a spoonful of whipped cream.

> Serves 10-12
> *First choose which fruit you would like to use and prepare:*
> *About 750 g of fresh fruit:*
> *Plums (pitted and halved) or*
> *Apples (peeled, cored and sliced) or*
> *Fresh gooseberries or*
> *Blackcurrants or redcurrants (topped and tailed) or*
> *Rhubarb (sliced) (see photo)*
> *or 750 g fruit from a jar or tin (drained weight!):*
> *Pitted sour cherries (the German supermarkets might sell them)*
> *Apricot halves*

Grease and bottom-line a 26 to 30 cm diameter round cake tin or pie dish.

Preheat oven to 180 C (350 F) static/160 C (325 F) fan/gas 4-5.

> *Now make the cake mix:*
> *200 g soft salted butter*
> *175 g caster sugar*
> *1 egg*
> *1 tsp vanilla essence*
> *300 g plain flour*
> *100 g ground almonds*
> *2 tsp baking powder*

Cream fat and sugar together with an electric mixer until pale and creamy. This will take about 2 minutes. After this, add egg and vanilla essence while still mixing on high speed. Put the mixer aside.

Sift the flour and baking powder into a separate bowl, add the ground almonds and mix together with a hand whisk.

Pour this into the fat, sugar and egg mix. Using a spatula or large spoon, mix the flour into the fat. Once it gets lumpy, use your hands to lightly work the dough into small crumbs. This is a sticky mixture, not pastry but rather a heavy sponge mix.

Take out about one-third of the crumble mix and put aside.

Turn the rest into the prepared cake tin and press gently into the base of the tin. Don't worry about working the dough up the sides of the cake. If using juicy fruit like rhubarb or gooseberries, scatter a handful or two of breadcrumbs on top of the base now.

Follow by scattering the fruit evenly on top, then crumble the reserved cake mix on top.

Bake in the preheated oven for 40-50 minutes (or longer if using a ceramic pie dish) until golden brown.

Leave to cool for at least 15 minutes before turning out of the tin. Dust with icing sugar before serving.

Breton butter cake (optionally GF)

Another treat from France, introduced to me by my lovely French friend Claire, fantastic boss and mentor during my time at the Argyll Hotel. It's a great way to use up those egg yolks you have left after making meringues (I often freeze the yolks and use them later). The cake is a mix between shortbread and a sponge cake – softer than a biscuit, but not as spongy as a pound cake.

Although it was made originally with a mix of buckwheat and wheat flour, I am using only wheat in this recipe for a lighter, more universally liked flavour, though the gluten free version still suggests using some buckwheat flour.

Have this wonderfully simple cake with a strong cup of coffee!

Serves 6-8
4 large egg yolks
160 g plain wheat flour
(for a gluten free version: 80 g plain GF flour
and 80 g buckwheat flour)
160 g salted butter
160 g caster sugar

Preheat the oven to 190 C (375 F) static/170 C (340 F) fan/gas 5. Grease an 18 to 20 cm diameter round baking dish (or 15 to 18 cm square tin) and line with baking parchment.

Place the very soft butter into a bowl, add sugar and, using an electric mixer, whisk for 2-3 minutes on high speed until pale. Add the egg yolks and mix until well combined.

Put the mixer aside. Sieve the flour into the butter mix and fold in with a spatula until just combined – do not beat or mix too long or the cake will be heavy.

Spread into the prepared tin, score with a fork and also scrape a few lines on top, criss-crossing each other.

Place into the preheated oven and bake for 15 minutes, then turn the heat down to 170 C (375 F) static/150 C (300 F) fan/gas 3-4 and continue for a further 15-20 minutes – you want the cake to be golden on top, and a skewer inserted in the middle to come out clean.

Once baked, take it out of the oven, and leave to cool for 5 minutes before cutting it into pieces. Leave to cool fully before removing from the tin.

Serve dusted with icing sugar.

Cranberry and coconut picnic slice (GF, optionally DF)

I like to call this traybake a 'posh Bounty'. While those little bars might always be the last ones to be picked from your chocolate selection box, this slice will not remain long in your cake tin.

Makes 12-16 small pieces
170 g dark chocolate (min. 50% cocoa solids)
90 g salted butter (or dairy free spread and a good pinch of salt)
145 g caster sugar
165 g fine desiccated coconut
(if you only have medium, whizz for a few seconds in your food processor)
90 g currants, though other vine fruit will do too
90 g dried cranberries
2 small eggs

Preheat your oven to 170 C (340 F) static/150 C (300 F) fan/gas 3. Line a 20 x 30 cm or 25 x 25 cm tray with baking parchment.

Heat up about 1.5 cm of water in a small pan. Place the chocolate into a metal or heatproof bowl (bigger in diameter than the pan), place over the boiling water and melt the chocolate while stirring occasionally.

Scrape the melted chocolate onto the parchment-lined tray and spread out in an even layer so that the whole base is covered. Place in the fridge or a cool place to set – this will take at least 30 minutes. Do not rush this process.

In a bowl, cream together sugar and softened butter with an electric whisk for 2 minutes on high speed. Add eggs, one by one, while mixing, then put aside the mixer. Add the coconut, vine fruit and cranberries and fold in by hand until well combined.

Spread over the set chocolate base. Bake for 20-30 minutes until lightly browned on top and set in the middle.

Leave to cool fully on a cooling rack away from heat or sunshine – this will take 2 hours or more. Once cold, lift the slab out of the tray, by holding on to the overhanging bits of parchment, onto a large chopping board. Cut into 3 x 4 or 4 x 4 rows, pressing hard to make sure you cut through the chocolate layer. Enjoy – these are perfect for afternoon tea, a school fete or a day in the hills.

Vegan lemon and poppy seed cake (VEGAN, optionally GF)

An easily and quickly made cake – we love its refreshing nutty lemon taste.

Serves 6-8
210 g self-raising flour (wheat or gluten free)
150 g caster sugar
¼ teaspoon salt
Zest of 1 unwaxed lemon
250 ml dairy free alternative to milk
Juice of ½ lemon
1 tbsp poppy seeds
70 ml sunflower oil
1 dessertspoon apple cider or white wine vinegar
1 tsp vanilla essence

Optional icing:
90 g sifted icing sugar
1 tbsp lemon juice

Grease and paper-line an 18 cm cake tin. Preheat your oven to 180 C (350 F) static/160 C (325 F) fan/gas 4.

Into a bowl sieve flour and baking powder, then add caster sugar, seeds and salt. Mix well with a hand whisk.

In a jug, combine oil, zest of lemon, vinegar, vanilla and dairy free milk alternative.

Make a well in the dry ingredients and add half of the liquid to it, slowly drawing in the flour mix bit by bit. When quite thick, add the rest of the liquid and mix fully without over-beating it. The cake mix will have the texture of thick batter.

Pour into the prepared tin, place into the oven and bake for 30-40 minutes or until a skewer inserted in the middle comes out clean. Leave to cool on a cooling rack before turning out.

Make a thick glaze by mixing sifted icing sugar with about 1 tbsp lemon juice and spread it over the cooled cake.

Delicious on its own or with some fresh berries on the side, this makes a good pudding or cake for afternoon tea.

Lemon shortbread biscuits

These are often our 'Welcome bake' biscuits, offered to arriving guests. Light and crumbly, substantial and so good in their simplicity. They only really taste right made with butter.

> *250 g salted butter*
> *125 g caster sugar*
> *250 g plain flour*
> *125 g cornflour*
> *Zest of one unwaxed lemon*
> *Demerara sugar for sprinkling*

Preheat the oven to 150 C (300 F) static/130 C (265 F) fan/gas 2. Line two large baking trays.

Wash the lemon and zest finely using a microplane. Place zest into a bowl, along with the very soft butter and caster sugar, and cream together using an electric hand mixer on high speed until pale and fluffy.

Add both the flours, and on the lowest speed mix them until just combined.

Sprinkle extra flour onto a flat table surface, place shortbread mix on top, sprinkle lightly with more flour, and roll out to 1 cm thickness. Cut out round biscuits, about 6 cm in diameter, and place on the lined trays, leaving 1.5 cm between each. Sprinkle each biscuit with some demerara sugar.

Bake for 30 minutes. Rest on trays for 10 minutes before transferring to a cooling rack.

Once fully cooled, store in an airtight container.

Our 'Abbey crunch' biscuits (optionally GF and/or VEGAN)

You will love these simple, satisfyingly crunchy biscuits. Add little extras like 2 tbsp each of pumpkin seeds and dried fruit like currants or cranberries for a more substantial cookie.

Makes 18-20
110 g salted butter (or dairy free spread and a good pinch of salt)
1 tbsp honey or golden syrup
150 g plain flour (or plain gluten free flour)
125 g soft brown sugar
75 g porridge oats
½ tsp bicarbonate of soda

Preheat oven to 200 C (400 F) static/180 C (350 F) fan/gas 6. Line two large baking trays with parchment or a reusable liner.

In a small pan gently melt butter and honey.

Gather all dry ingredients, including any extras you would like to add (see introduction), in a bowl.

Add liquid to the dry ingredients. Mix until a sticky dough has formed. Shape into walnut-size balls and place on the baking trays 5 cm apart to leave room for spreading.

Bake for 10-15 minutes until golden brown and the balls have spread into round biscuits. Let them rest for 10 minutes before transferring to a cooling rack. Once cooled, store in an airtight container.

Scones (optionally DF)

Nothing like a fresh, light, crumbly scone with butter and good jam! They are easily made, but just consider these simple rules: don't overwork the mix, work swiftly (baking powder once mixed with liquid will lose its rising power if left for too long) and put them in a preheated hot oven.

Though best eaten on the day they are made, they freeze well, and are almost as good as freshly baked if warmed through for 5 minutes at 180 C (350 F) static/160 C (325 F) fan/gas 4-5 or half a minute in the microwave.

Makes about 10
500 g self-raising flour (white or a mix of wholewheat and white)
125 g butter or dairy free spread
½ tsp salt
50 g caster or soft brown sugar
200-250 ml milk or a dairy free alternative

Preheat your oven to 220 C (425 F) static/ 200 C (400 F) fan/gas 7 – if this takes longer than 10 minutes, then start the preheating well before the baking process.

Get your equipment and cutting-out area ready: a large baking tray dusted with some flour, a round pastry cutter, about 5 cm in diameter, and a place for rolling out the dough, dusted with flour, plus a wee pile of extra flour on the side.

Place self-raising flour, fat, salt and sugar into a bowl. Work the fat into the flour using the tips of your fingers and thumbs. The mixture should, when finished, resemble fine breadcrumbs.

Add 200 ml of the milk all at once to the bowl, and using a dinner knife combine the mix with a few quick movements, cutting through it rather than stirring. If it seems too dry and crumbly, add a bit more milk – you will need more liquid if you use wholewheat flour. It should have quite a moist consistency but not be runny.

It is really important not to knead the mix – kneading develops the gluten in the flour. While this is important for bread, where we appreciate and love the chewy texture, it would produce heavy scones that hardly rise.

Using a spatula or similar, shape the mix into a lump in the bowl and scrape out onto the previously floured kitchen surface. Dust with some more flour. Roll out or just use your hands, pressing lightly until 3 cm thick.

Dip the cutter into the wee pile of flour on the side (this will prevent it getting too sticky) and start cutting out scones, placing them onto the floured tray, leaving at least 2.5 cm space in between so air can circulate during the baking.

Combine the leftover bits of mix without too much kneading, adding a little bit of liquid if necessary to stick them together, and continue to cut out scones until all the mix is used up.

Place the baking tray immediately into the hot oven and bake for 15-17 minutes until golden brown. Leave to cool for a little before breaking one open to have as a treat!

Scone flavours to add:

- 60 g dried fruit – we love cranberries, raisins and finely chopped apricots
- finely grated zest of one unwaxed lemon and 1 tbsp poppy seeds
- 1 tbsp treacle mixed with the milk before adding
- 30 g finely chopped crystallised ginger

Buckwheat, banana, date and walnut loaf (GF, DF)

A very satisfying loaf – not too sweet, perfect for tea break or as a snack on a good hill walk.

I usually freeze bananas when they have gone beyond edible – just peel them and place into a bag or a tub with a lid, and freeze. Defrosted, the bananas will not be a pretty sight, but the freezing process will have made them even sweeter.

Makes 1 loaf
250 g buckwheat flour
1 tsp baking powder
1 tsp bicarbonate of soda
½ tsp salt
3 large overripe bananas, about 350-380 g peeled weight
170 g runny honey (melt gently in a small pan or microwave if it has set)
1 egg
75 ml sunflower oil
150 g chopped dates
125 g walnuts
80 g pumpkin seeds

Preheat the oven to 170 C (340 F) static/150 C (300 F) fan/gas 3. Grease and paper-line a large 900 g/2 lb loaf tin.

Sieve flour, baking powder and bicarbonate of soda into a large bowl. Add the salt too and mix well.

In a separate bowl, mash the bananas with a fork or with an electric hand mixer.

Add vanilla, eggs, honey and oil, and mix well with the electric mixer or a handheld whisk.

Add wet mixture to the dry ingredients and fold in. Now add walnuts, seeds and dates and mix them in too.

Pour into the bread tin and even out.

Bake for around 1 hour 10 min to 1 hour 30 min or until a cake skewer, inserted in the middle, comes out completely clean. Cool on a rack before serving.

Keep for up to 5 days in an airtight container, or slice up and freeze, with a piece of parchment between each slice to enable defrosting a slice at a time (on a low setting in the toaster works really well!).

Sweet yeasty swirls

These have become a firm favourite on Iona, especially during the Covid lockdowns of 2020, when we had baked goods for sale (for home delivery during lockdown, and later in the Community shop) every Friday.

It's the cinnamon swirls that people are probably most enamoured with; however I will also give you other filling suggestions which are just as tasty.

By making the yeast dough the day before and leaving it in the fridge to rise overnight, you should have fresh swirls by lunchtime the next day.

> Makes about 14 swirls
> *350-380 ml lukewarm milk*
> *500 g strong white flour*
> *1½ tsp dried yeast*
> *½ tsp ground cardamom*
> *½ tsp salt*
> *50 g caster sugar*
> *Zest of ½ unwaxed lemon*
> *55 g melted butter*

In the afternoon or evening of the day before:

Place flour, cardamom, yeast, salt, sugar and lemon zest into a mixing bowl. Add most of the milk, about 350 ml, and using an electric mixer with a dough hook, a food processor or your hands, mix the ingredients together to form a sticky, not too firm dough. Add more milk if the dough feels dry.

If using a machine, knead for 7 minutes. If not, turn the dough out onto a surface and knead by hand for 10 minutes.

After this, melt the butter gently without heating it up too much. Add to the dough and mix until fully incorporated. This will seem like hard – almost impossible – work, especially if you are kneading by hand (you might want to pop the dough back into a bowl for the first part of it!). However, after 4-5 minutes (sooner with an electric mixer), instead of a slippery mess you should have a smooth, shiny, soft dough.

Place dough into a large plastic lidded food box with plenty of space for it to expand (at least double), or into a bowl covered with a plate, and leave it in the fridge.

Overnight, the yeast in the dough will have time to ferment and slowly cause it to double in size.

The next morning:

Take the dough out of the fridge and let it come back to room temperature for about an hour.

Preheat your oven to 200 C (400 F) static/180 C (350 F) fan/gas 6. Line two large (40 x 30 cm) baking trays with parchment.

Decide on your filling (see below) and get ingredients ready.

On a lightly floured surface roll out the dough into a rectangle about 30 x 40 cm in size, less than 1 cm thick.

For cinnamon swirls: 80 g butter, melted; 3 slightly heaped tbsp soft brown sugar and 1½ tsp cinnamon mixed together.

Using a pastry brush, spread the melted butter on top of the dough, then sprinkle the sugar cinnamon mix evenly on top.

For tahini, lemon and white chocolate swirls: Combine 3 heaped tbsp tahini, 2½ tbsp caster sugar, juice and zest of one washed, unwaxed lemon into a sticky mix. Scrape the tahini mix onto the dough and, using a spatula or the back of a tablespoon, spread evenly up to each edge. Sprinkle 100 g of white chocolate (drops or chopped) on top.

For walnut and dark chocolate swirls: 80 g butter, melted; 3 slightly heaped tbsp soft brown sugar; 150 g walnuts, finely chopped or ground; 100 g dark chocolate (drops or chopped).

Using a pastry brush, spread the melted butter on top, then sprinkle sugar, walnuts and chocolate evenly all over it.

Taking hold of the longer side of the dough, roll it up tightly into a roulade.

Using a sharp knife, cut into 3-cm-thick slices and place onto the prepared trays at least 3 cm apart. This way they will not fuse together but remain as individual pastries.

Cover with tea towels and put in a warm place. After 40-50 min the swirls should have doubled in size – leave them longer if they haven't.

Place into the hot oven (both trays if you have a fan oven, one after another for static or gas ovens, to make sure the buns get good heat from bottom and top). Bake for 9-13 minutes.

During the baking, make a sugar syrup by boiling together 60 g caster sugar and 60 ml milk. Get a pastry brush ready.

Once the swirls are out of the oven, brush with the hot sugar syrup, transfer to a cooling rack and leave to cool.

The swirls are gorgeous when still slightly warm, and really are best eaten on the day they aremade. However they do freeze well, and are almost as good as fresh once toasted or warmed up in a microwave or oven.

NB Savoury swirls: A lovely twist to the above, great for lunch or a picnic. Use half the amount of plain bread dough (see page 21), roll out and fill it with pesto, olive tapenade or grated cheese and thyme, roll up and cut into swirls. Place 3 cm apart on a large baking sheet, lined with baking parchment. Leave to rise for 45 min in a warm place, then bake in a preheated oven for 9-13 minutes at 200 C (400 F) static/180 C (350 F) fan/gas 6.

Rock buns (optionally GF/DF)

Richer than scones with their extra content of butter and lots of fruit, these do not need jam when served. They are quick and easy to make, and are great if you need to make something for afternoon tea at short notice.

A good recipe for kids to try out.

> Makes 15
> *300 g self-raising flour (wheat or GF)*
> *170 g of dried fruit (A mix containing mixed peel is great, but really it's your choice)*
> *75 g soft brown or caster sugar*
> *½ tsp cinnamon*
> *150 g soft salted butter or dairy free alternative*
> *2 small eggs*
> *(½ tsp salt, if using dairy free spread rather than salted butter)*

Preheat your oven to 190 (375 F) static/170 C (340 F) fan/gas 5. Grease two baking trays (or line with baking parchment).

Whisk up the eggs in a small jug or bowl. Put aside.

Place flour, sugar, salt, cinnamon and soft butter into a bowl. Use your fingers to work the fat into the flour until it all resembles fine breadcrumbs.

Add the fruit and mix in. Get a big spoon or spatula, pour the egg over the flour mix and mix briefly until just combined – you want to achieve a crumbly texture of lumps, not a large piece of dough.

Using two spoons put golf-ball-sized blobs onto the baking trays, 5 cm apart. Place immediately into the preheated oven and bake for 15-18 minutes until light brown. Leave to rest on trays for a few minutes (the buns are a bit fragile at first) then transfer to a cooling rack. They can be eaten as soon as they are no longer hot – and are probably at their best then.

Drinks

Hot chocolate with orange and cardamom (GF, optionally DF)

We have often made this hot chocolate on Easter morning for worshippers returning from the sunrise service – the perfect drink when one feels a bit 'chilly at the edges'.

For 2
500 ml milk or dairy free alternative
2 heaped tsp cocoa powder
2 level tsp honey or soft brown sugar
A strip of orange zest
3 cardamom pods

Wash an orange, first by placing it into a jug and pouring hot water over it to melt off any wax. Dry with a tea towel, then cut off a long strip of the orange layer, trying to avoid the white pith which is bitter.

Place this and all the other ingredients into a heavy-based pan, whisk to combine, then heat up slowly until steaming (but not boiling! – that will change the taste of the milk), giving the orange peel and cardamom pods time to infuse. Taste before serving – add more sugar or honey if you like it sweeter, and remove the peel and cardamom pods.

Serve in two of your favourite mugs.

A cup of tea

There's nothing like a good cup of tea! It wakes you up early in the morning, refreshes you after a long day's work or travel, relaxes you in the evening, and can even soothe heartache.

Most people obviously know how to make 'a cuppa'. However, I am including this because my family and colleagues do like to tease me about the care and meticulousness I put into making my daily cups of tea.

Serves 1

Get your favourite mug, a small saucer and a tea bag (I love Clipper). Fill the kettle with about 400 ml water and start the boiling process. When it is almost at the boil, pour hot water into the mug until halfway full. Cover with the saucer. Put the kettle back to boil.

Once it has boiled, pour out the water which has preheated the mug, put in the teabag and pour boiling water over it. Place the saucer on top of the mug again. If you have a very cold kitchen (the Abbey kitchen can be quite chilly on a winter's morning) wrap a tea towel around the mug.

Set the timer for 6 minutes. When it goes off, fish out the teabag, add a substantial amount of milk, and enjoy. There is nothing like the first sip of strong milky tea in the morning!

Turmeric drink (GF, DF)

For thousands of years treasured in Ayurvedic medicine, turmeric is known for its anti-inflammatory and antioxidant properties. When one of us on the kitchen team seems to be threatened by a cold I will offer up the following concoction which has in many instances helped to keep the lurgy at bay.

Serves 1

1 level tsp honey

1 tbsp freshly squeezed lemon juice

1 lightly heaped tsp ground turmeric

1 level tsp freshly grated ginger

A good pinch of ground pepper or chilli (the piperine in both helps the body absorb turmeric's active ingredient, curcumin)

½ tsp of sunflower oil or any other not too strong-tasting oil (again, this helps with the absorption)

Place all above ingredients into a mug. Add some hot but not boiling water from the kettle, enough to make ⅓ to ½ a cup of liquid. Mix, leave to cool a bit, then drink quickly – it won't taste amazing, but hey, it's meant to be medicine, not a pre-dinner drink!

Freya's quick egg and miso fix (DF)

I often used to make this instant soup for my daughter when she came to the Abbey or home for lunch from primary school here on Iona. Warming, tasty, nourishing. If you should have some cooked greens, e.g. broccoli or kale, left over from last night's dinner, add them for substance.

Serves 1

½ tsp vegetable stock powder, e.g. Marigold Bouillon

1 egg

Boiling water from the kettle

1 tsp miso paste

Into one large mug (which can comfortably hold about 350 ml of liquid) place half a teaspoon of vegetable stock powder and the egg (and any leftover cooked greens if at hand). While filling it up with about 300 ml of boiling water from the kettle, stir vigorously into a 'snowstorm' – this will cook the egg.

Add a teaspoon of miso to the broth, stir well until dissolved, then drink or spoon while eating your favourite sandwich.

Thank you!

My special thanks go to four amazing women who really put me on the path I am still treading today:

My mother Karin and my Oma Hilde, who both taught me to make delicious food with simple, fresh ingredients. I sat in their kitchens from an early age, watching and tasting, long before making a dish of my own.

Usch Koehler, who encouraged me to be both creative and relaxed in cooking: 'Just check out the contents of your fridge and throw it together!' Usch and her family welcomed me like a daughter to their home – I will forever be grateful for that.

Helen Lambie taught me – besides many, many other things – to make light scones! Thank you for being a great teacher, and believing that I could be an Abbey Cook.

In no particular order, my appreciation goes out to many more:

Thank you, all cooks, deputy cooks and kitchen volunteers who worked at the Abbey and the MacLeod Centre, for the joy and hard work you brought to this place – you really made it all work!

Thanks to Annie Sharples, Debbie Ryman, Clare Sibley, Nikhita Pandian, who have cooked with me (and hopefully will again) and who have also proof-read this book and tried out its recipes. You have been great companions.

Alison Holmes – for being a treasured colleague, adviser and friend.

Claire Bachellerie and Dan Morgan, you taught me a lot (not just cooking-related) while working at the Argyll Hotel. Your big hearts and generosity will stay in my memory always. Claire, I will forever remember your sparkling eyes when eating good food, whether a simple soup refined with an extra drizzle of olive oil, or fresh Scottish oysters.

Neil Harvey, always positive, and full of energy and good ideas – what a great team we were at the St Columba Hotel! Living the dream!

Linda Cameron, the lightness and joy you display when cooking for hundreds in an under-equipped village hall kitchen is so inspiring. You are a star!

I am so grateful to all my dear friends on Iona and Mull who fed me amazing food, introduced me to new dishes, let me cook in their kitchens, lent me ingredients last minute, gave me challenges and offered mental support and practical help. You are all amazing!

To my brother Ronny and his family, Nora, my cousin Uta and hers, my dad, my aunts and uncles – I am so grateful to you for keeping a strong link with me despite being hundreds of kilometres away.

To my Scottish sisters- and brother-in-law and their families, who from the beginning welcomed me with open arms and open houses. You are a great bunch and I love you lots.

Last but not least, my gratitude and love to my husband Mark and daughter Freya, to Neil, Isla, Elsie and Corrie, to Stewart, Rebecca and Laurie – how wonderful it is to have a family.

Books mentioned in the recipes

Bread Matters: The state of modern bread and a definitive guide to baking your own, Andrew Whitley. Fourth Estate, 2006.

Some recipes from various Cranks recipe books inspired Abbey cooks before me. I inherited their notes and adapted the recipes.

Other books which might be useful to you

My cookbook shelf is constantly expanding. While I use the internet a lot for recipe research, I do prefer browsing through books, leaving notes in the margins of the pages.

The following is a selection of food-related books which have inspired me over the years with their recipes and writings:

A Modern Way to Cook, Anna Jones. Fourth Estate, 2015.
Cooked: A Natural History of Transformation, Michael Pollan. Penguin Books, 2014.
Darina Allan's Ballymaloe Cookery Course, Darina Allan. Gill Books, 2007.
Jerusalem, Sami Tamimi and Yotam Ottolenghi. Ebury Press, 2012.
Falastin, Sami Tamimi, Tara Wigley. Ebury Press, 2020.
Food DIY, Tim Hayward. Penguin Books (Fig Tree), 2013.
How To Be a Domestic Goddess, Nigella Lawson. Random House (Chatto & Windus), 2014.
Made in India, Meera Sodha. Penguin Books (Fig Tree), 2014.
Mary Berry's Baking Bible, Mary Berry. BBC Books, 2009.
One Pot, Pan, Planet, Anna Jones. Fourth Estate, 2021.
Palestine On a Plate, Joudie Kalla. Jacqui Small, 2016.
Salt, Fat, Acid, Heat, Samin Nosrat. Canongate, 2017.
Spoonfed, Tim Spector. Jonathan Cape, 2022.
The Diet Myth, Tim Spector. Weidenfeld & Nicolson, 2016.
The River Cottage Fish Book, Hugh Fearnley-Whittingstall and Nick Fisher. Ten Speed Press, 2012.
World Food Café, Chris and Carolyn Caldicott. Frances Lincoln, 2002.